BY THE EDITORS OF CONSUMER GUIDE®

MODEL TRAINS

Beekman House

New York

Contents

This edition published by:
Beekman House
A Division of Crown Publishers, Inc.
One Park Avenue
New York, N.Y. 10016

Library of Congress Catalog Card Number: 79-64870
ISBN: 0-517-294621

Introduction

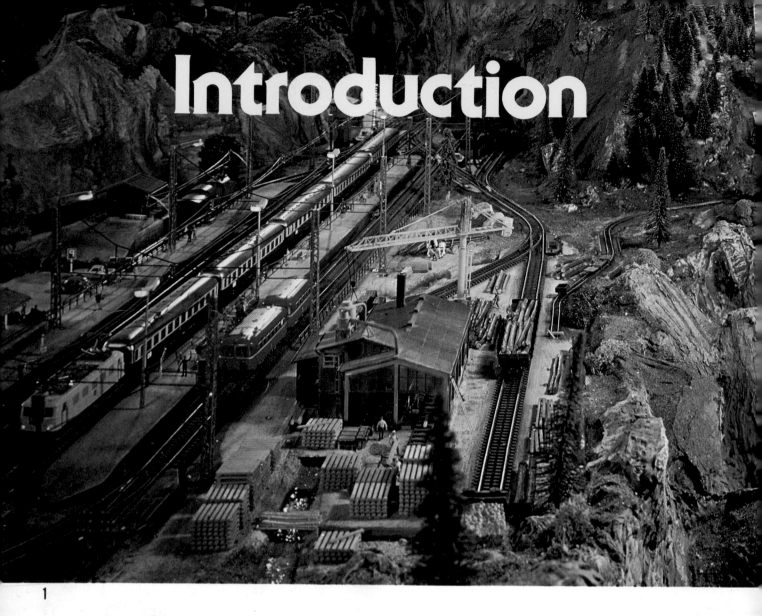

1

THE FACT THAT model railroading is very popular today is not surprising—not when we consider the illustrious history and tradition of the great trains, not when we think of the romance and excitement that railroads have engendered in so many people over the years.

The lonely wail of a train whistle somewhere off in the distance has long been the symbol for people traveling, going to and coming from faraway places. Its plaintive cry was once as compelling a call to inland residents as a ship's whistle was to those who lived near seaports and harbors. The engineer behind the controls of the roaring locomotive was as much a folk hero as any ship captain.

For much of this century, and part of the century before it, trains were the principal method of transporting people, mail, raw materials and finished products. The locomotives were awesome, powerful machines capable of great feats: they pulled scores of freight cars loaded with thousands of tons of every kind of commodity from milk to coal. The cars were elegant: the private coaches of the Vanderbilts, Astors and Carnegies rivalled the most opulent parlors of Fifth Avenue and the living quarters of the most fabulous yachts. Railroads were important: these lifelines of commerce and industry ran from one ocean to the other; across the Great Plains, over rivers and through mountains.

As faster forms of transportation developed, however, the railroad's role in commerce and travel shrank. Big trucks now roll down superhighways, carrying goods that once were hauled crosscountry by train. Airliners now whisk travelers from New York City to Los Angeles in the time it would take a train to cross a single state. Parlor cars like those of the Astors and Vanderbilts are gone. The Orient Express has made its last journey.

This is not to say that railroads are dying. They still play an invaluable part in worldwide commerce. Thousands of commuters ride trains from

The range of activities open to the model railroader is vast. Hobbyists work on what are called "lifetime layouts" over many years, such as the one represented by Marklin's mountain environment (1). Others spend countless hours assembling and decorating all types of structures like the tin shack from Campbell Scale Models (2). Some modelers buy certain locomotives because of their historical significance. Among the models sold by Bachmann are replicas of the Union Pacific locomotive (3) and the Central Pacific Jupiter (4) two trains that came together upon completion of the world's first transcontinental rail line--when the Golden Spike was pounded into place.

2

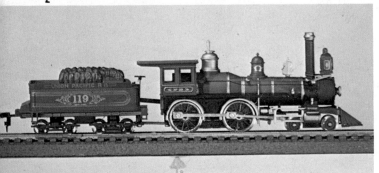

3

4

their homes to work every day, and thousands more travel by train just for the fun of it. Modern railroads continue to carry countless tons of cargo back and forth across the United States and most other countries of the world.

Although many people would not consider railroading today to be as glamorous and romantic a mode of transportation as it was 50 and more years ago, there are innumerable railroad enthusiasts everywhere who preserve the past and celebrate the present by building and operating replicas of trains and the worlds in which they travel. MODEL TRAINS is dedicated to model railroaders and railroaders-to-be.

The Hobby's Beginning

Model railroading is practically as old as railroads themselves. The history of miniature replica trains, in fact, can be traced all the way back to the 1830s: some 15 years before Chicago, the city Carl Sand-

burg called the "player with railroads," the city that was to become the world's greatest railroad center, saw its first real train; more than 30 years before the Golden Spike united the Union Pacific and Central Pacific lines to complete the first transcontinental railroad.

Model railroading was not a hobby back in the 1830s, but that was the decade when the first true miniature railroad was built. Mathias Baldwin, founder of the Baltimore Locomotive Works, crafted a small model of a locomotive and several passenger cars as well as an area of track. His creation was not for entertainment, however; it was a design model for a locomotive he was planning to build. That first model locomotive served its purpose well. Its design was used in the building of "Old Ironsides" for the early Baltimore & Ohio Railroad.

In the beginning, miniature trains were built only to serve as design models. The locomotives and cars were explicitly detailed to resemble what the

Modelers who enjoy assembling kits will find a wide range of them to choose from. Bowser makes many kits, including the Old Lady steam-powered locomotive and detailed coal car.

manufacturer planned to build. They were painstakingly constructed of hand-tooled metal and hand-crafted wood—often a combination of both —and the more elaborate ones were powered by miniature steam engines.

Train sets were first introduced as toys around 1900. The hobby that model railroaders know today, however, did not really get underway until the mid 1930s when motors and electrical systems became readily available. But as soon as model railroading began to catch on as a popular new hobby, it was just as quickly curtailed by World War II. The nation turned its attention away from model trains and other toys.

After the war, however, the hobby had a rebirth and grew at an amazing rate until about 1950. Then television became an integral part of the American leisure scene. Many hobbyists abandoned their model trains to watch Milton Berle and Ed Sullivan. But the novelty of television began to wear off, and people began to return to other pursuits. Among them was model railroading. In recent years, the hobby has seen a continual and impressive growth.

Model railroading should be differentiated from the simple act of hooking up and playing with electric train sets. The latter may be the way potential modelers are introduced to the world of miniature trains, as children or as adults. But true modeling is a craft, a truly creative effort. It is the reproduction in scale of trains; track; related equipment like signals, switches and spurs; and all the accompanying elements such as scenery, structures, and everything else necessary to re-create in miniature a total railroad environment. It may represent the real world or be something that springs from the modeler's imagination.

There are approximately a quarter of a million serious railroad modelers in the United States today, a number that does not include the uncounted thousands who simply break out the old train set every Christmas and perhaps add a new item or two each year. The serious modeler is a year-round train buff who steadily works at the hobby, who builds or fashions his or her own layout and the environment in which the railroad will be set. The model railroader is the person who has made a true commitment to the hobby in terms of time, effort and money.

The state of the craft today is the grandest it has ever been. More people than ever before are involved in model railroading; more sophisticated equipment is available; more hobby stores and mail-order dealers offer products, tools and supplies; more publications are on the market; and there are more clubs, activities and competitions being offered to modelers now than at any other time.

The wide variety of equipment today is offered by a large number of manufacturers, both American and foreign. From molded plastic to hand-crafted brass, there are trains for every level of interest and every budget. There are settings and environments as simple or as elaborate as you could want.

The Range of Activities

The reason why the hobby's popularity is strong and continually on the increase is that model railroading offers as much or as little as the hobbyist wants to put into it. It can begin with nothing more than setting up a basic model train set that comes with everything in a single package. It can develop into the unending process of building unique trains and environments, refining them, altering them, extending them. It can lead to competition on a regional, national, even international scale. The hobby takes people down different paths.

In model railroading, one person may want his freight train to run through a city or town environment; another equally dedicated hobbyist would prefer to have a passenger train tunnel through mountains or cross over a simulated river on a two-foot-tall trestle.

There are various sizes of trains and accessories

to suit varying tastes in model making. Model locomotives can be more than a foot long or small enough to fit into a walnut shell. Locomotives and cars are readily available in all of the standardized sizes, either ready-made or in kits to be put together. The most ambitious and skilled modelers build from scratch. All of the various environmental features can also be bought preassembled or be built by the modeler. Houses, train stations, shrubbery and trees, human and animal figures, mountains, trestles and tunnels can be bought or constructed.

Throughout the country today, there are many clubs where model railroaders get together, work together and compete against one another with their craftsmanship. The national organization that oversees and coordinates so much of the model railroading activities, the National Model Railroad Association, currently lists more than 25,000 members and is growing every year. National, regional and local conventions are held annually and model railroading news is disseminated monthly.

Today, in basements, playrooms and garages all around the country there are incredibly elaborate layouts that required years to build and set up.

These miniature cities, mountains and desert scenes resulted from the creative efforts of model railroaders from various walks of life. Many of their builders began with simple electric train sets; then ventured beyond that and began putting together something of their own.

They were beckoned by that whistle's wail; stirred by visions of steam engines hauling their loads through frontier America, troop trains taking men and their weapons to battle, the vista-domed Burlington Zephyr gliding through the majestic mountains and canyons of the West, of politicians campaigning from the backs of trains in whistlestop towns across the country. These modelers were enthralled by tales of intrigue on the Orient Express and the legend of Casey Jones.

MODEL TRAINS tells you how to get started in the hobby and how to move ahead in it. It provides some tips to help you succeed, and guides you to additional sources of help and to the makers and distributors of the products you will need. The train that will take you on an exciting journey around the world of miniature railroads is ready to depart.

All aboard!

A Model Die Casting kit, assembled and finished by an expert, displays the artistry of authentic detailing.

Getting Started

1

FOR SOME CHILDREN, a visit to Grandma's house is the beginning of a lifetime of fascination with model railroading. Rummaging around in the attic amid the musty, dusty boxes and stacks of yellowing newspapers, the kids may find a rusting train set. Other children receive their first train sets as Christmas presents, or as hand-me-downs from friends or relatives who have progressed to more advanced equipment.

A recent poll by *Model Railroader* magazine determined the two most common reasons why model railroaders take up the hobby. One reason is simply that the hobbyist has always liked trains; the other is that the adult modeler owned a model train when he or she was a child.

If you are not already a model railroader, or if you know someone who would like to find out how to get started, one of the most important first steps is to visit a hobby shop and get an idea of all the equipment that is available. There you will see the vast assortment of products and be able to compare them and their prices. Also, a novice model railroader usually can pick up some free guidance and advice from the hobby store's owner or manager, who very often is somewhat of an expert on the subject.

2

3

The assembly and finishing of a kit like the Pennsylvania 2-8-0 from Roundhouse Products (1) requires the skills of an experienced modeler. Many expert hobbyists began with simple train sets, such as those from Lionel (2). Bachmann also makes a variety of train sets for beginners (3). These sets --with locomotive, cars and power equipment all in one box--are a good way to get started.

Other helpful sources of valuable information are the manufacturers of model railroading equipment. Many of them publish catalogs containing descriptions of their products and other facts that can be beneficial to the beginner. Local clubs also can provide help in getting started. Hobby shop personnel may be able to direct you to a club in your area.

The idea is to collect as much information as you can about this far-reaching hobby before you spend any money. Do you want to become involved with the hobby as a collector only, a modeler only, or both? The collector's chief interest is in owning and displaying replicas of trains. The modeler is a person who wants a complete train setup and layout (which in most cases requires designing and building one), and wants to put the tiny locomotives and cars into opération in the miniature environment. Most modelers eventually become collectors as well.

If modeling is your choice, you'll have to decide what type of train setup you want to begin with. The simplest form is a packaged set, one that contains all the basic elements: locomotive, cars, track, power supply and wiring. Some of these sets are nothing more than simple toys; others are much more sophisticated. Even if one of the more ad-

A broad area of the model railroading hobby is the assembly and decorating of miniature cars, or rolling stock. One company that makes many different types of cars is Model Die Casting. MDC's cars are sold under the Round-house name. Among them are the three-window caboose (1) and Hi-Side ore car (2). Those modelers who do not want to construct and paint their own cars can buy them ready to roll.

vanced sets is chosen, it will serve only as a jumping-off point. The modeler, to deserve that name, must move on from there; adding or replacing parts, developing a truly unique layout.

Locomotives, cars and all the other pieces you may need or want for your model railroad system can be bought ready-made or in kit form. They can also be built from scratch. Setups can be, and often are, the results of a combination of these methods. This opportunity for creativity and craftsmanship is what keeps model railroaders interested in the hobby for a lifetime.

Scale and Gauge

As in other hobbies revolving around miniature replicas, an important consideration in model railroading is that of scale. The more realistic model trains are built in exact proportion to the prototype, or the full-size original. When models are built to scale, whether they are trains, airplanes, cars, or army tanks, they are constructed so that one inch on the model represents a specific number of inches on the prototype.

If the scale is 1:48, for example, it means that one inch on the model represents 48 inches on the prototype. A full-size locomotive's wheel that is 48 inches in diameter would be scaled down to a wheel one-inch tall on the model.

There are 17 different scales listed by the National Model Railroad Association. Only six, however, are commonly available; and two of them, HO and N, are used by about 90 percent of all railroad modelers. Because HO and N are so popular, most of the equipment you will see at a hobby shop will be in these scales.

1

2

The selection of one scale over another is a matter of personal taste as well as the amount of space available to the model railroader for the layout. Model Power makes locomotives and cars in HO scale (1) and N scale (2).

N scale trains are about half the size of HO. There are many other scales available, from those twice the size of HO and larger to those that are much smaller than the tiny N scale.

HO, a scale of 1:87 (one inch on the model represents 87 inches on the prototype), is far and away the most popular scale. More than 75 percent of all serious modelers concentrate their efforts on HO. N scale is a relative newcomer to model railroading, having been developed and first marketed in the early 1960s. But N scale, about half the size of HO, is rapidly gaining in acceptance on the model railroad scene. The scale designated O is the largest scale easily obtainable. It is a scale of 1:48, which means a 48-foot locomotive reproduced in O scale makes a model one foot long. Layouts for O scale are often set up outdoors because they are so big. HO, which stands for half O, is the mid-size scale. Trains sold by LGB and some other companies are twice as large as O scale. A scale much smaller than HO is the Z scale—a scale of 1:220. Marklin makes Z scale trains.

Gauge is the measurement of a railroad track's width, from the inside edge of one rail across to the edge of the other. Just as the engines and cars of a model are made in proportion to the full-size train, the width of the track they ride on is proportional to that of the tracks used by railroads. The width set by the U.S. Congress as the national standard was 56½ inches.

Not all track in America was built to this government standard, although most of it was. In some instances, trains and track on which they ran were built smaller so the trains would be more maneuverable and better able to negotiate tighter turns. These railroads and their track, which usually measured three feet in width but were sometimes up to a foot narrower than that, became known as narrow gauge.

Model railroads are available in miniature ver-

Brass locomotive kits from Overland Models are examples of how elaborate model trains can be.

sions of both gauges. Narrow-gauge model railroads offer the same benefits to the modeler as the prototypes did in the real world of railroading: the ability to turn and handle tighter curves in restricted areas. This is an important factor if the modeler is severely limited in the area he can use to set up a track layout.

If the American standard gauge is chosen as the gauge of the model train, the width of the miniature track will vary according to the scale of the model. In HO scale, for example, the gauge of the model railroad track is about .65 inch (56.5 inches divided by 87).

The following chart shows how various model trains compare to one another and to the full-size prototypes in terms of gauge and scale.

CHART OF SCALE*

Model Railroading Scale	Proportion	No. Inches to One Foot	Track Gauge Inches	Millimeters
1-inch	1:12	1"	4.75	120.66
3/4-inch	1:16	3/4"	3.531	89.69
17/32-inch	1:22.6	17/32"	2.5	63.51
1/2-inch	1:24	1/2"	2.5	63.51
No. 1	1:32	3/8"	1.75	44.46
O$_{17}$	1:45.2	17/64"	1.25	31.76
O	1:48	1/4"	1.25	31.76
S	1:64	3/16"	.875	22.23
OO	1:76.2	.157"	.75	19.
HO	1:87.1	.138"	.65	16.5
TT	1:120	1/10"	.471	11.97
N	1:160	.075"	.354	9.
Z	1:220	.054"	.256	6.5
Narrow Gauge				
On3	1:48	1/4"	.75	19.06
On2	1:48	1/4"	.50	12.71
HOn3	1:87.1	.138"	.413	10.50
HOn2	1:87.1	.138"	.276	7.02

*Compiled from a STANDARD established by the National Model Railroad Association© 1977, printed with permission.

Cost Considerations

How much money will you have to spend to get started in this hobby? What will it cost you to develop a truly satisfying and impressive layout?

The answers to these questions vary from hobbyist to hobbyist. The amount of money you will spend depends entirely on what you decide you want from the hobby and how you want to go about achieving it. A collector can invest thousands of dollars in models; an ambitious modeler willing to really work at the hobby may create an elaborate layout costing several hundred dollars; and, of course, it is possible to make do with a much simpler setup.

Most of the cost of railroad modeling comes at the beginning when you are just getting started. That is the time when you will buy a locomotive ($10 all the way up to $400); a power unit ($15 to several hundred dollars); cars; track and track equipment; and perhaps some environmental decorations such as miniature buildings, landscaping materials, other vehicles and so on.

It is difficult to predict how much it will cost any single individual because there is such a wide variety of trains and accessories available in all price ranges. In a survey, modelers were asked how much they spend each month on their modeling activities. They gave widely varying answers, but the average was approximately $25 a month. This was the amount that very serious modelers were investing to sustain their hobby activities.

The best way to approach model railroading is to determine what you want or need to begin. A simple train set, for example, may cost you only $35 to $60. You may be able to fashion much of the environmental decorations from scratch at low cost. Then again, you may decide to build your locomotive and cars from elaborate kits. If that is the case, not only must the cost of the kits themselves be taken into consideration, but the cost of the necessary tools and other supplies must be added in also.

Once you find yourself in the area of sophisticated kits, cost can mount up rapidly. Many craft kits do not include the wheel assemblies—called trucks—of cars and locomotives. Experienced modelers who buy kits that do include the trucks often replace the original wheels with trucks they buy separately, because the quality of the trucks can have a great effect on the operation of the entire model railroad system.

Most modelers who build from kits spend a lot of time decorating their locomotives and cars. Painting, detailing, lettering and weathering require good-quality paint brushes and good paints.

Clearly, the more complex the kit and experienced the modeler, the more extensive will be the array of tools and supplies. Some model railroaders actually set up complete machine shops

Sophisticated layouts including many handmade environmental features such as trestle bridges (1) and forests made of hundreds of miniature trees (2) are the results of experience acquired over several years. The hobbyist's first train system often is much simpler-- a train set such as those made by Tyco (3), for example. Such inexpensive sets can be the foundation of elaborate systems, because extra cars, new locomotives and environmental materials can be added to them over the years.

so that they can machine their own replacement wheels and other metal parts. However, other modelers get by with just the bare essentials and manage to create attractive and authentic replicas. Some models require only two or three basic tools for completion; for others, you may need a wide assortment of tools.

1

2

3

The amount of building and modifying you plan to do will help you to determine the number and type of tools and other equipment you will need. The basics consist of the following:

Hobby knife
Files (flat, triangular, round)
Sandpaper
Tweezers
Eyedropper
Scissors
Screwdrivers
Needle-nose pliers
Scale ruler
Paint brushes and paints
Paint thinner

Toothpicks
Cotton-tipped swabs
Glues and adhesives

You may, however, need some or all of the following items, depending on just what projects you have in mind.

Scale converter
Jeweler's screwdrivers
Hobby saw
Hobby-size miter box
Rail-cutting pliers
Razor blades
Vise
Soldering gun

4

5

Train sets are available in all scales, from the very small Marklin Mini-Club sets in a scale of 1:220 to the LGB sets that are many times larger (2). Environmental features such as the buildings from Kibri (3) are made to match the different scales. Many expert modelers surveyed--those who painstakingly construct the expensive brass models from Overland (4), for instance --say they got started in the hobby by playing with simple little sets like those from Lionel (5). The hobby of model railroading is so wide that all budgets and all levels of skill can be accommodated.

Solder
Clamps
Hobby drill and bits
Scribers
Hobby wrench sets
Butane torch set
Airbrush
Weathering paints and pastes
Motor tools: drill with grinder and sander attachments, drill press, lathe

The hobby of model railroading has a large following. Publications, organizations and clubs abound. Whether the beginner wants advice on getting started or the experienced modeler would like some tips on detailed painting, someone who would like to help is usually nearby.

Assistance in shopping for a particular train set or kit, choosing a scale, acquiring a complete set of tools and putting a model layout into operation is readily available. And model railroaders enjoy exchanging tips as much as they enjoy building and running their trains. Very often the personnel at hobby shops are themselves model railroaders or know someone who is. For that reason, and because it is wise to get a good idea of all the types of products on the market before buying anything, we recommend a visit to a large hobby shop. Also, many manufacturers of model trains and related equipment are willing and eager to supply catalogs of their products to hobbyists—often at low cost or no cost.

Train Sets

1

AN EXPERIENCED railroad modeler could be expected to view boxed train sets in much the same way as a French chef would look upon canned gravy. But many modelers begin with train sets simply because this is an easy way to get started.

The wide availability and low cost of good quality, scale-model train sets entice many a modeler. These sets offer an ideal base on which to build a much more intricate and expensive model railroad system. Today's train sets should be viewed not with disdain, but in terms of the very real merits they offer a beginning model railroader.

When we speak of a train set, we are referring to a single package that contains all the basic components, ready-made and ready-to-run, that make up a model railroad: locomotive, railroad cars, track, power pack and electrical connections. All you have to do to put a set into operation is break open the package, lay the track, position the train on it, and plug it into an electrical outlet.

In past years, when most of today's railroad modelers were still growing up, the toy world offered a number of marvelous electric train sets—most notably the three-rail, O-scale models produced by Lionel and American Flyer. Often purchased as Christmas gifts, they were brought out of the closet and set up only during that holiday season each year. These sets were generally sold and used only as toys. They were, however, enjoyed as much by adults as they were by children. The youngsters often would have to wait while fathers and uncles played engineer. These sets tantalized the would-be modeler, hinting at how much more could really be accomplished with a little ingenuity and a little more money.

Today, Lionel (now a division of Fundimensions) still manufactures train sets. American Flyer, however, has gone the way of Burlington Zephyr and is only a memory. But there are a number of other manufacturers who are marketing an interesting variety of model train sets in various sizes.

Some sets on the market are still classified and marketed primarily as toys. These include some of the very elementary sets produced by Lionel, Jouef and Tyco Industries. (Jouef, incidentally, offers an interesting toy set with a locomotive that runs on clockwork power instead of electricity.) Many other sets are manufactured in standard scales with realistic two-rail track systems by such respected firms in model railroading as Marklin, Bachmann, Atlas, and Life-Like Products. Lionel, Jouef and Tyco also offer elaborate sets in scale.

HO is by far the most common scale in which model railroad sets are manufactured today. This is also the scale of most accessories and replacement parts for subsequent additions or refinements to a system—something you will want to keep in mind if your ambitions go beyond simple toys.

There are sets in scales other than HO. Lionel, for example, still manufactures a set in the large O scale just as it did years ago. Near the other end of the size spectrum, Marklin offers a tiny Z-scale set and a variety of locomotives, cars, decorations and other accessories. Bachmann produces sets in the

2

3

5

The choices available to the model railroader in the area of train sets are many, from sets that are little more than toys to those that are fairly complex and realistic. Among them are Bachmann's Amtrak Express (1); Tyco's Rock Island Line (2); Bachmann's Old West Overland Freight (3); Lionel's Cargo King (4), Logging Empire (5), and Santa Fe Double Diesel (6); and Tyco's Santa Fe Action Freight (7). The companies that make these train sets also make additional cars, track sections, locomotives and mechanical accessories. These products enable the hobbyist to enlarge the sets as desired. Such sets are often purchased as gifts, because everything that is needed to put the train system into operation is included in a single box.

4

6

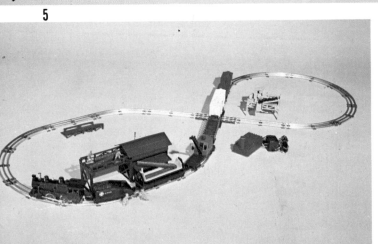

7

1

2

newly popular N scale for those who want to work in a size smaller than HO but not one as small as Z scale.

Complete sets sold by LGB (as well as separate components for advanced modelers) are made in a scale twice as large as O scale. This means that a railroad locomotive that is 40 feet long would be reproduced as an LGB model 20 inches long.

Expanding a Set

An ordinary model train set will contain only the basics: a locomotive; several railroad cars, usually three or four, but sometimes as many as seven or eight; enough track to construct a small oval layout; a relatively simple power pack, which generally provides only enough power to handle the needs of the set it comes with; and perhaps an accessory or two like a tunnel or crossing signal.

If the set is in scale, especially a popular scale like HO or N, there is almost no limit to the environ-mental scene that you can create by adding scale buildings, landscaping, vehicles, figures, track ac-cessories and so forth—all of which can be bought individually. Large hobby shops offer a broad se-lection of products in this area.

Track that comes with the set can be expanded by adding sections. You may want to enlarge the basic oval provided in the original set into a double oval or into a variety of other configurations. You will have to be sure, however, that your set's power pack is strong enough to accommodate whatever track and cars you add to your set. Generally speaking, you will have to upgrade the power pack as you expand a basic train set.

Model railroad sets, unlike the systems that mod-elers create for themselves, are designed to be set up, taken down, stored and set up again. The man-ufacturers are aware that most of the purchasers of their sets are not interested in setting up and main-taining a permanent system. You can, of course, make a set permanent by securing it to a table or

No matter which scale the model railroader wants, there are numerous train sets to choose from. Tyco is one of the many companies that make train sets in HO scale. One of Tyco's sets includes a billboard that produces the sound of a train whistle (1). Model Power makes several sets in N scale (2). Lionel's line of sets and accessories includes mechanical features such as drawbridges (3), and a variety of cars such as box cars (4) and livestock cars (5). In choosing a set, it is wise to consider all options, because a carefully chosen set can become the basis for a large and intricate layout. Some people who buy train sets, however, are not interested in expanding them. Instead, these trains serve only as toys and are not usually set up permanently.

3

4

5

large sheet of plywood; but you probably will not want to limit yourself in this way. It is much easier to expand on a system that is not literally nailed down. You would do well to decide just how you may want to expand on the simple oval and what kind of environmental scene you may want to create before you make your system permanent.

When buying a train set, just as when purchasing any model railroad item, it is wise to take a good look at what is available. Shop carefully, comparing various types of sets, because there are some major differences in quality of materials and construction, as well as in price. A well-stocked hobby shop ordinarily carries a selection of model railroad sets; toy and department stores often handle good scale-model sets along with toy trains.

Determine first what you want to do with a set; that is, what purpose it is to serve. Will it be a holiday season setup only, a permanent system that will stand as is with perhaps only a few environ-mental additions, or one that will serve as a base to

build on over a period of time? Look for a set that will enable you to accomplish what you have in mind.

Once you have decided on a particular set, examine it thoroughly in the store if you are allowed to, or as soon as you get it home. Most stores will let you open a box and examine what is inside before you purchase the set. A demonstration model set up in the store will show you how the system operates, but it will not tell you exactly what is in the box you intend to buy and the condition of the parts.

When inspecting a set, be sure all elements are in the box and that they appear to be unused. Make certain that an instruction booklet or sheet is enclosed. Determine exactly the amount of space the system will take up in the configuration you are planning. Check the trucks on the cars, making sure the wheels spin freely and uniformly and that the trucks themselves swivel easily. Examine the locomotive carefully for any loose or missing parts, misaligned wheels, faulty wheel movement or cosmetic flaws.

You will have to wait until you get your set home to give the system a more thorough inspection and an on-track test. You should do that immediately. The longer you wait, the more difficult it might be to get replacements from the store. A locomotive that does not run properly can ruin an entire system, and a faulty or underpowered power pack may not be strong enough to operate the crossing gates and signals you wish to add to your system. The track may not hook up properly. These are all

Realizing that many owners of train sets will want to expand their systems, Tyco makes a Layout Expander, including the "terrain," track and wiring (1). It contains everything needed to expand any circular HO track into a system designed to accommodate two trains. Bachmann's Rail Blazer train set includes a double oval track, six cars, a locomotive and an oil tank that produces the sound of a diesel horn (2). Bachmann makes a wide variety of cars, locomotives, buildings and mechanical accessories that allow the hobbyists to enlarge any Bachmann set little by little.

1

2

problems that could be discovered at the very outset of your model train operation, when adjustments can be made by you or the dealer.

That brings us to another important point: Be sure your dealer is one who will stand behind the merchandise he sells. Some stores may refuse to replace defective parts or take back flawed train sets. Established hobby shops, on the other hand, very often are run by people who are themselves model railroaders. They sincerely want to help the beginner and the experienced hobbyist obtain as much enjoyment as possible.

1

2

One of Bachmann's larger train sets is Railroad City (1), complete with five cars, locomotive, track, structures and street signs. A small set designed for children is Lionel's Workin' on the Railroad, which includes an operating log dumper car and a loading mill (2). A much more realistic set is Bachmann's Budd Metroliner (3). This set, decorated to resemble an Amtrak commuter train, gets its electric power from the track rails, so it is intended for use with "dummy" cables strung over the track.

3

Locomotives and Cars

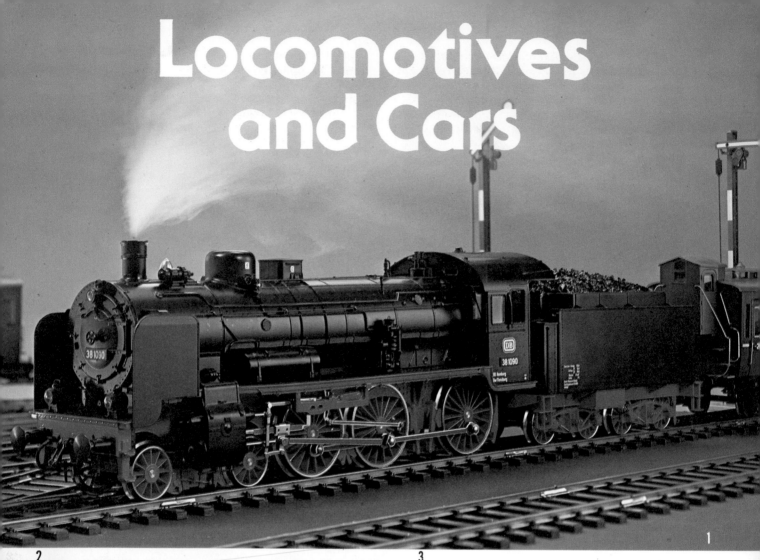

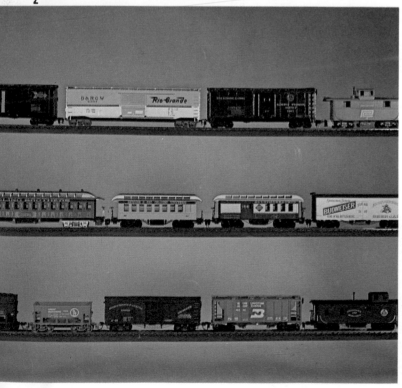

2

3

1

BANDITS IN A Hollywood Western watch the clouds of black smoke on the horizon and listen for the thunder that tells them the payroll train is nearing their ambush. In a large American city, automobile traffic waits for a commuter train to clatter past, its electrical contacts skipping along the wires overhead, crackling and sparking. Elsewhere, travelers line up to board an Amtrak train as its mammoth diesel idles with an eardrum-rattling hum.

These huge machines have similar work to do—to pull cars full of people or cargo—but they differ in operation and size. So do miniature locomotives used by model railroaders. Much of the excitement of rail travel revolves around the locomotive. An appreciation of the engine's power seems to come naturally to everyone. The excitement of model railroading also is produced by the locomotives. To pull long chains of cars along a hobbyist's track, these little engines must be powerful for their size.

Much of the drama of a railroad system is generated by the type of engine pulling the train: its appearance, its capabilities, its performance, its uniqueness and its compatability with the overall setup. One modeler we spoke with describes the locomotive as the single element that "puts life in a model setup and really brings home the realism."

Some modelers want trains that reflect the past: a steam engine, maybe, pulling a long line of classic Pullman cars; those splendid cars with open platforms at either end and interiors of a plushness

long gone from the tracks of America. Others may want to re-create the present, with two or three diesel engines working as a team to pull contemporary freight cars; or perhaps a sleek passenger train, shaped for speed and efficiency. Whichever you choose, much of your model railroad's character will be created by the locomotive and cars you select.

The area of broadest choice is that of the cars. The cars, referred to in railroader's jargon as the rolling stock, are the full-size train's reason for being. They carry the cargo: sleepers full of people, freezers full of beef sides, and racks of brand-new automobiles. There are four basic categories of rolling stock: freight cars; passenger cars; cabooses; and the maintenance-of-way cars, or, as they are known to railroad personnel, M.O.W. (Some railroaders make no distinction between a caboose and an M.O.W., because both are "riders" that produce no revenue for the railroad.)

In the freight-car category, there are at least 10 types of rolling stock: box cars, refrigerated cars called reefers, livestock cars, tank cars, ore cars, flatbeds, logging cars and circus cars among others. In the passenger-car class also, the assortment is large. Coaches, Pullmans, observation cars, diners, baggage cars, and new bi-levels are available to the modeler. Maintenance-of-way rolling stock includes derrick cars, cranes, track-laying equipment, snow plows and other cars that carry machines for repairing and maintaining railroads. Some of the models of these railroad cars are quite

4

5

A huge assortment of model locomotives and cars are available in kit form or ready to roll. Among the preassembled engines and cars marketed worldwide are those from Marklin (1) and Bachmann (3,5). Detailed kits are sold by Model Die Casting under the Roundhouse name (2,4). All scales, price ranges and degrees of authenticity are easy to find. Any era of railroading can be represented by the locomotives and cars sold by the numerous manufacturers--from the days of the first Iron Horse right up to the powerful diesels of the present.

simple; others are highly detailed. There is great freedom for modelers to use their ingenuity in refining, modifying and customizing. Cabooses, too, offer many challenges to the modeler, especially in detailing and decorating. Have you ever seen a caboose without the scars of weathering and rugged use? There are many different types of cabooses that have trailed trains along the rails of the world. They are often unique in their design, in their specified functions, and in the way they look as a result of the work they've done and the places they've been.

Locomotive Types

There are three basic types of power used by full-scale locomotives: steam (usually generated by a coal-burning boiler), diesel fuel and electricity. Since most model trains run on electricity, the important difference between the three types of full-size locomotives as far as the modeler is concerned is in the way they look. Steam locomotives are very popular because of their classic styling and the nostalgia they generate. Diesel and electric locomotives are of more recent vintage. Their exteriors are smooth and aerodynamic. The selection of one over the other influences all the other parts of the train setup, because buildings, cars and other accessories used must reflect the era of the locomotives.

Since full-size steam locomotives are in use now only as symbols of the past, the decorations used

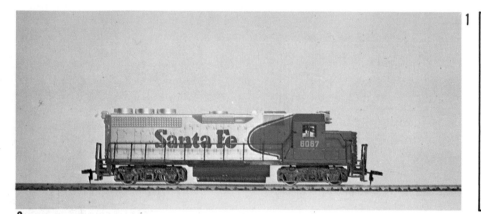

1

Whether the modeler wants to design a train system around a modern diesel engine like those available from Bachmann in pre-assembled from (1) or a locomotive from the early days of railroading like those made by Model Die Casting in kit form (2), the choices are endless. The MDC Roundhouse kit is a hand sample --specially decorated by an expert modeler. It and the Bachmann are HO scale models.

2

with model steam engines usually are designed to look like the scenery of the 1800s. On the other hand, models of diesel and electric engines look modern and are used in modern-looking environments.

The long and glorious history of trains is of great interest to most collectors and modelers. Down through the years, intriguing systems were developed to classify the various types of locomotives, and those classifications can be used by a modeler today in selecting one miniature locomotive from the numerous designs available.

For steam locomotives, which include everything from small switchers—the tugboats of the rail yard that are used to move cars from one track to another—up to the powerful freight haulers, the basic classification system of the more than 40 types of engines is called the Whyte Locomotive Classification System. Named after F.M. Whyte, the mechanical engineer of the New York Central and Hudson River Railroad Company who devised the classification many years ago, it identifies the locomotive type by the number of wheels in the three sets each steam locomotive has. In the designation 4-6-2, for example, the first numeral is the number of front or pilot wheels; the second numeral signifies the number of drive wheels; and the third is the number of wheels at the rear.

Most types of steam engines also have been given names. The most well-known of these locomotives and the ones most commonly built by modelers are:

Common Name	Whyte Classification
American	4-4-0
Atlantic	4-4-2
Berkshire	2-8-4
Consolidation	2-8-0
General	4-4-0
Great Northern	4-8-4
Hudson	4-6-4
Mikado	2-8-2
Mogul	2-6-0
Mountain	4-8-2
Northern	4-8-4
Pacific	4-6-2
Prairie	2-6-2
Ten-Wheeler	4-6-0

Diesel locomotives, using internal-combustion engines of the type first developed in the 1890s by German engineer Rudolf Diesel, were introduced to the railroad industry in 1934 and very quickly made the steam locomotive obsolete. Today, all locomotives except electric ones are diesel powered. Diesel locomotives have their own classification system, using a combination of letters and numerals. The letters refer to the number of drive axles and their wheels.

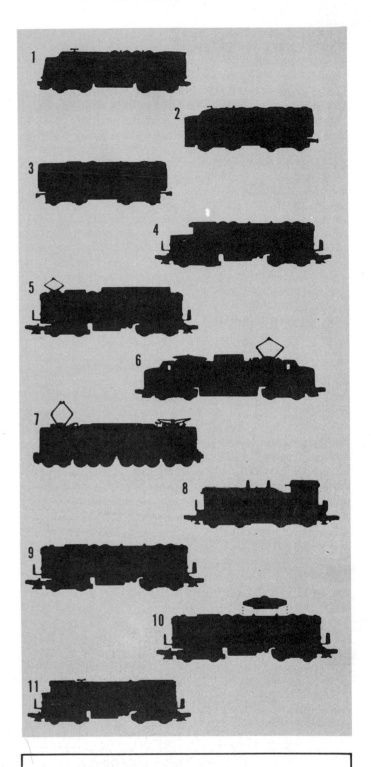

The ability to recognize the various types of diesel engines is part of the fun of model railroading. Lionel's catalog contains silhouettes of 11 different diesels. They are the F3 (1), Alco A (2), Alco B (3), GP-20 (4), Rectifier (5), Electric (6), GG-1 (7), SW-1 Switcher (8), GP-7 (9), GP-9 (10) and U36B (11). In addition to these names, diesel locomotives also are known by a combination of numerals and letters that designate the number of drive axles and wheels that all of them have.

A: one drive axle; two wheels.
B: two drive axles; four wheels.
C: three drive axles; six wheels.

Numerals used in this system denote free-running axles—those not connected to a motor. A model of the Santa Fe diesel Streamliner, like the one in HO scale offered by Marklin, would be designated BO-BO because the front truck has two drive axles and no free-running axles—BO—and the rear truck is the same. The classification A1A-A1A indicates that the front truck has one drive axle with two wheels, one free-running axle, and another drive axle with two wheels; the rear truck is a repeat of that configuration.

Like steam engines, diesel locomotives are identified by type. The most familiar, perhaps, is the F-3 which is often referred to as the Streamliner. Here is a list of the 11 most common types of diesel locomotives: Alco A, Alco B, Electric (electric diesel), F-3, GG-1 (electric diesel), GP-1, GP-9, GP-20, Rectifier (electric diesel), SW-1 Switcher and U36B.

Electrically operated trains are more common in Europe than in the United States, except for urban or interurban transportation. They are not classified by any widely used system. There are, however, two basic types: locomotives that receive electrical energy from a third rail on the track; and those that obtain power from overhead cables.

A special term is given to some types of electric trains by the National Model Railroad Association: traction. The NMRA defines traction trains as "all equipment particularly associated with urban, suburban and interurban railways, electric powered."

Models in this group are treated as a completely separate category for judging in NMRA-approved competitions. *Model Railroader* magazine estimates that more than 12 percent of all serious model railroaders in the United States today are also avid builders of traction models. As a matter of fact, there is an entire magazine devoted exclusively to the hobby of building and operating traction models: *Traction and Models Magazine.*

The term traction comes from the type of electric motors used by these railway vehicles. Such traction motors were first introduced to America in the late 1800s. The power to drive the motors comes from either third rails or from contact overhead.

Model Locomotives and Cars

Model engines can be costly: those made of brass, hand crafted and extremely detailed, sell for hundreds of dollars. But some that are mass-produced and made of plastic cost $15 or less. Many other model locomotives that are bought ready-to-run or in kit form, or built from scratch, are available at prices between these two extremes. This is the range from which most modelers select their locomotives. One nice thing about model railroading is that unless you are in it only for collecting, you can effectively start out with an inexpensive locomotive and work your way up to the more expensive models.

For the ambitious modeler who enjoys building from kits, there is a great deal of satisfaction to be obtained from this pastime. Assembling an engine,

1

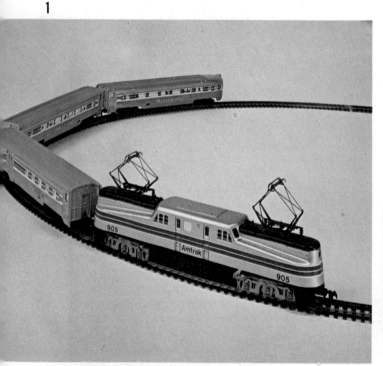

2

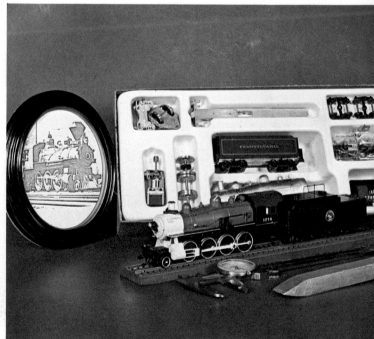

however, requires a good deal more patience, knowledge, skill and experience than it takes to assemble a train car. But if you feel ready to take on such a task, you probably will come away with a feeling of great accomplishment, and you may also save money. It is possible to save approximately half the cost of a ready-to-run locomotive by assembling one yourself. This is no minor consideration, especially when you want a good brass model.

When you have decided to make the transition from buying ready-to-run locomotives to assembling a kit, it is wise to start with a fairly simple one. One of the HO scale, 0-6-0 switchers from Roundhouse Products is simple enough for a beginner. In general, however, kits for rolling stock are easier to assemble than kits for locomotives. Experienced model railroaders suggest that novices begin their kit building with a relatively simple rolling stock kit, one that contains a small number of parts and requires a minimum of skill to put together. As we'll discuss shortly, there is much you can do to even a simple kit to increase its authenticity. Later, after you have acquired the necessary abilities and confidence, you can move up to a more complex car kit and then to locomotives.

Of course, you don't have to build a locomotive or a railroad car to be a model railroader. For hobbyists who look upon building and finishing as chores rather than fulfilling pastimes, ready-to-run locomotives and rolling stock are the things to buy. Most serious modelers, however, want a hand in the development of all elements of a railroad. This is why most model railroad cars and many locomotives are produced in kit form. The things that make a full-scale train unique are the things that make the building and finishing of even the simplest rolling stock kit an art.

Kits on the market today vary widely in terms of the materials used, the detailing of parts, complexity and price. Model railroad cars are made of metal, plastic, wood, or a combination of these materials. A good range of kits in practically all the standard scales is available. They are diverse in their difficulty. Some of the more advanced kits involve many more individual pieces and considerably more effort on the part of the modeler. A railroad car in this category can require days or even weeks of work to complete and the result is usually in direct proportion to the hobbyist's skills and experience. These elaborate kits are aimed at the truly serious modeler and are often distinguished by the term "craft kits." Other kits require as little as an hour to assemble. The simpler ones come with much of the detailing and paint decorations applied by the manufacturer, but these can be modified. The advanced kits leave all the detailing up to the modeler, and that is where the art comes in.

Few models of traction trains are available in preassembled form, and none of the kits for traction models are simple enough to be put together in minutes. Rather, the kits that are available require a solid commitment on the part of the modeler, and a lot of skill. Very often, traction kits include only the car's body, motor, electrical pickups and hardware and leave the building of other components up to the modeler's ingenuity.

3

All the different types of locomotive power are represented in models. Tyco makes a train set modeled after the Amtrak electric locomotives (1); Model Die Casting makes a Roundhouse kit of a steam engine (2); and another Tyco set includes a model of a modern diesel locomotive (3). Many expert modelers recommend that beginners start with an inexpensive locomotive such as those found in complete train sets and gradually work their way up to kits such as those from Roundhouse. There are many kits that provide a real challenge to even the most experienced modeler. For those hobbyists who want to get their train systems underway quickly, however, many very realistic locomotives and cars are sold in ready-to-run form.

Assembly, Painting

We cannot begin to tell you how to build a model locomotive or rolling stock kit because the parts and assembly steps vary so greatly from one kit to another, but we do have a few hints that may prove valuable. They are simple, and based on common sense.

Just as you would do with a kit of any other type, check to make sure all the pieces are included in the box after you open it. Use the enclosed instruction sheet to familiarize yourself with all of the parts before you begin assembly. Read the instructions carefully to make sure you understand every step before you begin. That way, you will not find yourself stumped by an unclear step when your model is only half finished. Be sure to keep the instructions in a safe place during assembly and afterwards. You will want to refer to them later when you need to clean, lubricate or repair the locomotive and cars.

Once you begin assembly, take your time. Move step by step, carefully following the instructions. At various times during assembly, it may be necessary to stop and test the locomotive on the track to be sure that its moving parts are working properly.

Painting and weathering are two important steps. It may be necessary to paint some items before assembly. Other painting techniques vary according to the materials used by the model manufacturer. (If the locomotive is made of brass, for instance, you will have to soak it for several minutes in a solution that will enable the paint to adhere properly to the metal, then rinse it thoroughly in water before painting.)

Such companies as Testor, Floquil, Pactra and Scalecoat offer a huge variety of paints for model railroading. What you will want is a thin paint, one that will not obscure details. That is the characteristic of paints made specifically for modeling. Applying the paint smoothly is up to you, however. Be sure all areas to be painted are clean and free of dust or other particles. The best method of painting is with a smooth brushing technique. Use only the highest quality brushes for this, like the pure red sable brushes from Grumbacher. The results of spray painting are not usually as uniform as those you would achieve with careful brushing. Always be sure when you finish painting to thoroughly clean your brushes; it is one way to hold down the costs of your modeling. Good brushes are not cheap.

Putting the letters, logos, trademarks and other identifications on a piece of rolling stock is another important facet of the hobby. These elements can be transferred to the model in either of two ways: wet or dry. Wet decals are the easiest to apply, but they are not necessarily the most realistic in appearance. In addition, the decal film around the area of the transfer can detract from the model's appearance. There are ways to avoid this (prepainting the area with a specialized clear paint for that purpose—usually available at a hobby shop), but it may be better to develop the skill of dry decaling. Dry letters are transferred from a sheet to the model by being rubbed onto the model with a stylus-like implement called a burnishing rod

1

2

Among the Roundhouse Products locomotive kits that are available from Model Die Casting are those of the Southern Pacific T-28 (1) and the narrow-gauge Baldwin Consolidation (2). A large choice of rolling stock--all preassembled--is made by Lionel for use with the company's toy train sets (3).

(available at art, hobby and craft stores). The result is usually very realistic. Whichever way you go about lettering and applying the decals, be sure to finish the job by spraying the area of transfer with a coating of transparent paint.

Weathering is the ultimate in detailing and the master touch of an expert modeler. Battered by dirt and dust, rusted by rain and snow, and bleached by the sun, trains quickly take on a weather-beaten look. A brand-new train on a track in an otherwise naturalistic setting seems out of place. To achieve realism, you will have to treat your train to achieve results similar to those of the elements. This is the method modelers generally refer to as weathering. It requires skill and artistry that are learned and developed through practice and experience.

The first step in weathering is planning, deciding just what you want to render: rust, dirt, stains, scratches and streaks. Look at photographs of full-size trains and note the kinds of weathering that are clearly visible. Or examine the real thing if that is possible, and perhaps take your own photographs for later reference. It is from sources like these that you will find the perfect guide to realism.

Floquil is one company that produces special paints for weathering purposes. They are appropriately named Rust, Mud, Grimy Black, Dust, etc. These can be brushed or sprayed directly onto the railroad car. It will take some practice and experimentation to achieve the best results. You may have to mix several paints to get the effect you want. It probably goes without saying, but we will say it anyway: Practice your painting for weath-

ering and test your colors and mixtures on something other than that nice model you have constructed.

There are also other materials besides paints that can be used for weathering effects: crayons, chalk, powders (talcum, graphite, etc.) and even fine-grain sandpaper.

Another technique for effective weathering is to use an airbrush — it will gently and thinly blow paint onto the railway car to produce some excellent effects. Airbrushes, good ones anyway, are expensive. An effective airbrush kit may cost $50 to well beyond $100. Badger, Bammco, Floquil and Paasche are well-known producers of quality airbrushes for the modeler. Airbrushing technique is an art. There are many books currently on the market that are devoted to this aspect of model building. If you invest a lot of money in a good-quality airbrush, you will surely want to put a few more dollars into some good books about its operation and technique.

Realistic rolling stock can add a great deal of interest to a model railroad system. Always keep in mind, however, that all the components of the total model railroad environment that you have created should blend together, just as they would in a real-life scene.

Building from Scratch

Modelers who work extensively with kits and kit materials often complement their efforts with some form of scratch building — detailing, customizing or adapting a particular design. A hobbyist can enhance his or her model by going beyond the pieces and instructions in a kit. The result will be a much more personalized model, and will often be a much more authentic replica.

There is less of a difference between assembling a kit and building from scratch than the word scratch may lead you to believe. Often, the distinction between the two is minimal. There are few if any hobbyists who can make every part of a locomotive from scratch. To do that, you would need an elaborate machine shop. Usually, hobbyists make some of their own parts and buy the others. Those who build from kits and have gained some experience often make their own modifications in subsequent kits by using raw materials.

The National Model Railroad Association has a term for the type of artwork often created by modelers who use kits. The term is "super detailed," and it has a precise definition. Such models are sophisticated in appearance as a result of many hours of detailing by the modeler. The NMRA says: "To be considered super detailed, it is necessary that a model have considerably more detail of excellent quality than usually expected. The quality of the detail is of more importance than is the quantity. But in the case of models built from kits the

3

term implies additional detail beyond that supplied with the kit.''

Some of these models are cross-kit models; that is, they are fashioned from the pieces in two or more kits. Others are modified by the modeler, using assorted bits of plastic and other materials to give the railroad car a look of authenticity far greater than that which could be achieved by using only the parts in one kit. Some are extensively altered to resemble a particular kind of car. Many traction kits not only allow scratch building, but require it. Many of the pieces needed to complete the model simply are not included in the kit.

Progressing beyond the level of super-detailed cars and locomotives are those that are built from scratch. Again, the NMRA has some specific guidelines that determine which models are eligible for entry into contests for ''scratchbuilt'' models. ''To be considered scratchbuilt,'' the NMRA says, ''a model must have been completely constructed by the entrant without the use of any commercial parts except items that a modeler could not fabricate himself. These include such things as the wheels, light bulbs, coupling parts and assorted wood, met-

The Roundhouse narrow-gauge locomotive rounds a bend in a mountain environment.

al and plastic shapes. Furthermore, the NMRA says, "The term 'scratchbuilt' carries the implication that the builder alone has accomplished all of the necessary layout and fabrication which establish the final dimensions, appearance and operating qualities of the scale model."

To accomplish their goal of extreme detail and watching resemblance of the model to the original railroad car or locomotive, many modelers collect photographs, drawings and even blueprints of the full-scale equipment. They research the history of railroading, reading about particular lines and the trains they used over the years. They investigate the types of materials used in the construction of the trains, the kinds of cargo they hauled and the other factors that would go unnoticed by all but the most devoted students of railroad lore.

An example of this is the amount of research and work that a modeler may do in assembling a detailed passenger compartment. The seats, the floor, the windows, ceiling, lights and other furnishings can take many hours to create. When finished, such a model is as much a tribute to the railroading industry as it is an example of the modeler's talent.

1

2

3

Some modelers buy their locomotives preassembled. LGB (1) makes a large assortment of locomotives for these hobbyists. For advanced modelers who like to assemble kits, superbly detailed brass kits are available from Overland Models (2). Bowser also makes kits of different locomotives (3). Many expert hobbyists often modify detailed kits by adding scratch-built features, after doing a great deal of research to be sure that the decorations are authentic.

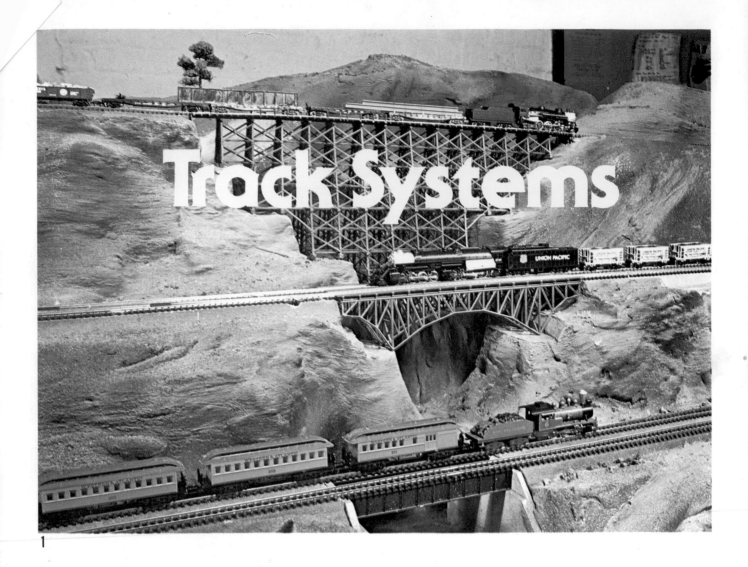

1

Track Systems

FOR YEARS, THE Santa Fe Super Chief has sped along track that measures exactly four feet, 8 ½ inches from the inside face of one running rail to the inside face of the other. In Europe, the Orient Express traveled over track of the same gauge, and so did trains that ran between Shanghai and Peking. In fact, approximately 60 percent of all railroad traffic in the world today operates on track of this width, which has become known as Standard Gauge.

Some say we can thank the ancient Romans for this standard. Two thousand years ago, when the Romans were building the roads across Europe, they designed the paving so that the ruts would fit the standard axle lengths of the wagons, carts and carriages of the day — about four feet, 8½ inches. Over the years in Europe and later in America, wagons continued to be built with wheels set that distance apart. When the first railroads were being planned, it seemed logical to build trains with a similar width. Track was laid to fit, and that is how Roman wagons set the standard for railroads of today.

There are other widths or gauges of track. Some have been less than two feet wide; others as wide as seven feet. Narrower gauges were often used where railroads were forced to negotiate a series of very tight curves, especially in mountainous areas. They have also been used in underdeveloped countries, because narrow-gauge rail is less expensive — at least initially — to lay. In the model railroad world, the standard gauge is represented in scale, as are narrow-gauge tracks.

Track is one of the single most important items needed for a realistic model railroad environment. A well-designed and well-laid track is a necessity for the effective operation of the entire model railroad system. Inadequate track can adversely affect the function of the train, causing everything from derailments to disturbingly noisy operation. Entire books have been written on the subject of model railroad track alone.

The National Model Railroad Association points out emphatically in its official *Directory of Information:* "It is an unfortunate truth that too many model railroads suffer from carelessly engineered and

2

3

hastily constructed right-of-way and track. The finest model equipment built can perform only as well as the track on which it runs will permit. Time and care spent in preconstruction engineering together with sound and careful construction will be repaid many times over in satisfaction gained from the troublefree performance of the models running over it. Remember that track, too, is a model."

Track work for the modeler can be an exercise in craftmanship and creativity. You can become as involved as you want to in the construction process. If building track is not the most enticing area of the model railroad hobby for you, you can get along well with snap-together sections and ready-made roadbeds. Or, if this is an area of the hobby in which you are very interested, you can begin from scratch.

Planning is the key to proper track laying, whether you will do all the building yourself or assemble factory-made sections. You must devise just where your model train is going to travel: you must design the configuration of track that you want and that will fit into the space you have available. You will

also have to plan the environmental features that you will use to enhance your system. What is the scene going to be—mountainous, desert, or city? How can the track be laid out to its best advantage in that kind of scene? How many switches, intersections, sidings and spurs will be used? What about bridges and tunnels?

To progress smoothly, the track-laying operation must begin with pencil and paper. Like an architect, you will need a blueprint of what will be built. That way, you can devise what is feasible for you and then list the precise steps necessary to move along effectively in the construction of the system, avoiding many problems.

Space Considerations

Much of what you can do will be dictated by the area you have to work in. That is, how much space can be allotted to your model railroad environment?

Where to put your model railroad layout is an important consideration. It can be the principal

Restricted to a long, narrow area, the builder of this layout nevertheless created a sophisticated, entertaining system.

factor in determining which scale you choose. If space is at a minimum, you probably will not be able to use an O scale layout. If the area is limited to a long, narrow rectangle, you probably will be thinking in terms of a small scale like N or Z.

For most layouts an area of at least 50 square feet is recommended. That may sound larger than it really is: a rectangle five feet wide and 10 feet long, or a square a little more than seven feet on a side. A layout does not have to be rectangular, but that shape is the most common. A rectangular shape utilizes space efficiently. Layouts built in a C or E shape, or those that run along the walls of a room, are also considered ideal.

Basements are the areas most often used for permanent layouts. According to the survey by *Model Railroader* more than half of all the layouts built by serious modelers are located in basements. The second-most-popular area is a spare room such as an unused bedroom or den, or a family room. Garages can be used, but they often are not heated or equipped with the necessary electrical outlets. Attics are a possibility, but unless they are insulated, they can be uncomfortable in weather extremes of heat or cold.

Basements and spare rooms are generally most suitable. They provide sufficient electrical outlets, and they offer other favorable conditions for working at your hobby as well as for displaying and operating your model railroad. If none of these areas is available to you for a layout, you may be able to use some sort of collapsible platform in other rooms of your home. Many types of tables that come apart and go back together again can be bought or built. Something on the order of a folding bridge table, but larger, is often used by model railroaders. Some modelers construct platforms that are hinged to a wall and swing up or down and out of the way. In some cases, a wide closet can be used to hold a hinged platform of this type.

The ideal height for a model train table is about 42 to 48 inches. Equally important, then, is the space above the table. There must be enough headroom—at least 30 inches between the layout and the ceiling. In small spaces, an oval layout often works best. As a way of illustrating the importance of planning, we'll pass along a little tip in using an oval: do not position it squarely within the confines of the board or table; angle it so that the straightaways of track are not parallel with the edges of the surface. The overall visual effect will be less static and more natural and you will have two large areas at the corners to use for environmental features.

The variety of configurations is unlimited. The choice is a personal one, depending on factors of budget, space, and individual likes and dislikes. The NMRA, however, defines the following as the basic forms of model railroad designs and layouts.

Around-The-Room Railroad: a layout built against all walls of a room.

Canyon Railroad: a variation of the Walk-in Railroad where some or all the scenery extends to the floor, making the aisles into simulated canyons.

Dogbone Railroad: an elongated oval or lap with the tracks at the sides pressed together, somewhat in the manner of double track.

Fan Railroad: a layout with a main line that fans out to several destinations via different routes; can be point-to-point, out and back, and/or a loop.

Folded Dogbone Railroad: a dogbone type of plan in which the parts of the track are folded back until they overlap one another.

Lap Railroad: an oval layout in which the main line forms a continuous circle-like route of any shape.

Island Railroad: a railroad that is accessible from all sides.

Out-and-Back Railroad: a layout that has one principal terminal; the main line departs from the yard and returns by a different route, entering the yard at the point of departure.

Point-to-Point Railroad: a track with a main line that goes from one terminal to another, requiring trains to return via the same track; terminals usually have facilities for turning the train.

Shelf Railroad: a layout built against one or more walls of a room, normally protruding less than an arm's length from the wall.

Table Railroad: a variation of the Island Railroad, small enough so all parts can be reached from the outer edges; there are no internal or walk-in spaces.

Walk-in Railroad: a layout in which the aisles protrude into the body of the railroad and from which operations can be conducted; usually, all track can be reached from the aisles.

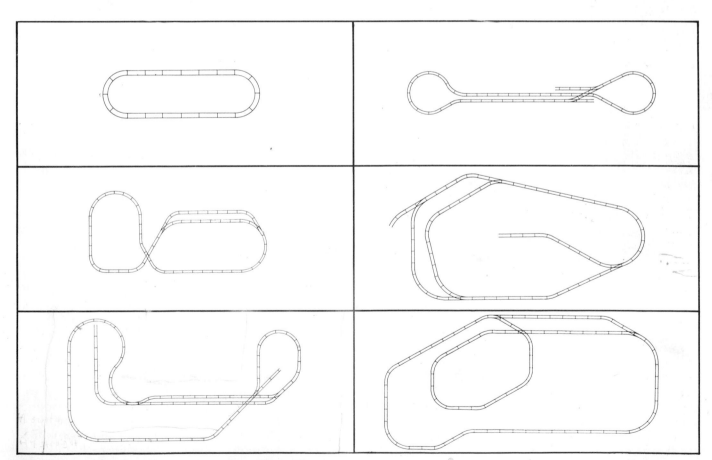

The variety of configurations for model railroad track layouts is unlimited. Basic forms (above) can be modified to suit a hobbyist's particular needs, desires and space considerations.

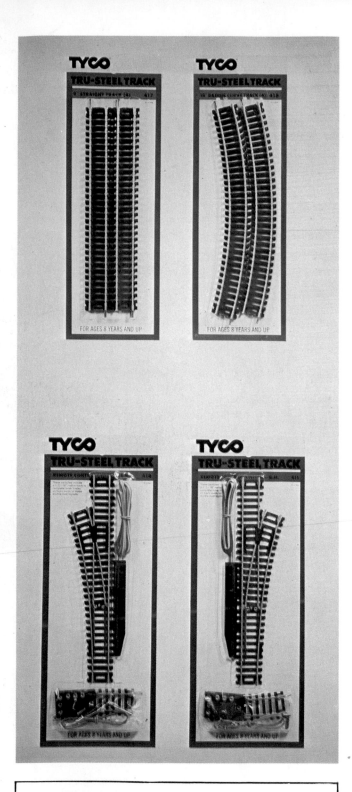

The enjoyment and creativity in this aspect of model railroading often comes from designing your own unique configuration. There are some basics you will have to take into consideration—such as the kind of track you will want to work with, the radius of turns, the limitations of your electrical setup and power pack—but designing your own track system is not difficult if you do some detailed planning and some experimenting.

If you decide to design your own configuration, you will want to take the following things into consideration.

● Determine how much space you will have for your layout: the area, and its shape; location in the house, and the limitations of that location.

● Decide on the type of track you will use: precut sections or flexible track that you can adapt.

● Calculate the maximum amount of track you will be able to lay in the selected area. Keep in mind the number of switches, crossroads, turn-outs and other such things that you will need.

● Prepare a full budget. The amount of money you can afford to put into the layout may restrict you to a smaller layout than you originally planned. If so, you will undoubtedly want to plan well, enabling yourself to add to the track later without having to tear up the entire system to do it.

● Experiment on paper with various configurations. Make a scaled-down drawing of what you want to accomplish. You will often find that what first seemed the best of all possible layouts can be improved upon with a little innovation.

● Add the environmental scene to your paperwork plan. Sketch all the roads, mountains, bodies of water, buildings, bridges and tunnels. You will probably have to alter and adjust your track scheme to fit the environmental scene as you go along. You may not be able to have everything you really want. Sidings may have to go to make way for the terminal annexes you want; the river you'd like to have "flowing" across your layout may have to wait until you can build a trestle.

● Make a full-size drawing, once you have the full design of your system complete in a scale drawing. This will enable you to discover any error or problem that may have eluded you in the small drawing, and a full-size drawing will also serve as an effective guide when you get down to actually laying the track.

● Take into consideration all engineering features. If you are going to bank your turns, you will have to plan for it.

● Determine what base you will use for your system. Tabletops work fine, but they are not as portable as plywood sheets can be. Remember that this base should not be something with a tendency to warp, sag or become otherwise deformed. If it is plywood, therefore, it should be at least a half inch thick; if it is pine, it should be quality grade.

● Assemble all the materials, supplies and tools that you will need.

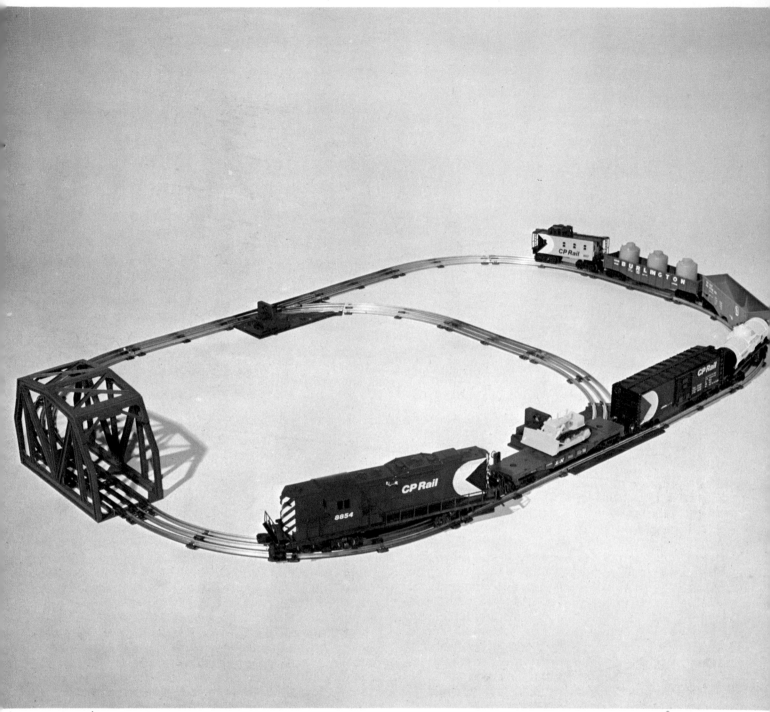

Lionel's track--having three rails instead of two--is not intended to closely resemble full-size track.

You are now ready to become a real-life gandy dancer (railroad construction worker), even if your rails, ties and spikes are a bit smaller than the real thing.

Realism in Model Layouts

Realism is a constant concern for the serious model railroader. Many modelers avoid simple track because it does not look realistic enough. This usually means more work on the part of the modeler, but the results are well worth the extra trouble.

The track sections sold by Lionel in its inexpensive train sets, for example, go together very easily. But those sections, which have three rails instead of two and have no authentic-looking ties, would not be acceptable in a layout that includes many realistic environmental items. The ex-

Exceptionally realistic results can be obtained by using sectional track like that from Hobby Marketing.

perienced modeler wants track that looks like real track. To achieve that look, some modelers fashion and lay their own track, tie by tie and rail by rail—often making the components from scratch.

Real railroads run on a roadbed, the layer of materials that forms the foundation for the track. For the model railroader, the train's roadbed can be simulated by homosote, a wallboard-type material available from lumber stores. Cork and wood can also be used. Full-size tracks also are ballasted; that is, the gaps between the ties, and under and at the sides of the rails are filled with gravel, stone, cinders, or other similar materials to facilitate drainage and to shore up the ties and rails. In model railroading, ballast is also laid down with track to make the layout look authentic. Material for ballast in most scales is available at hobby shops. Many kinds are prepackaged and ready to be glued to the track. Some do-it-yourselfers, however, grind their own ballast from a variety of materials.

Today, all the efforts involved with building from scratch are not necessary to achieve remarkable realism. Some modelers take great pleasure in working this way. Exceptionally realistic results can be accomplished by building every track component from scratch. But you can buy ready-made track in precut sections, in various curves to fit any layout. Some track sections have the roadbed built in; all you need to do is secure it to the base.

Laying, Maintaining Track

Laying track can be an intricate and tedious job or as simple as snapping together pieces as they come straight from the factory. Certainly, the latter is the easiest way. Sectional track, as it is commonly called, is readily available at hobby shops. (It is also the kind of track that comes in prepackaged train sets.)

Perhaps the two best-known types of sectional track are Atlas' Snap-Track and Tru-Scale's Ready-Track. Snap-Track comes in sections that simply snap together. The user must provide the roadbed and ballasting. Ready-Track, also in precut sections, comes complete with roadbed and artificial ballasting. As its name implies, Ready-Track comes already laid and ready to use.

There are other types of sectional track on the market. Some are simply lengths of rails and ties; others come in varying states of completion. Beginners usually work with sectional track, although many of the experienced modelers we talked with advise against it because of its limitations. Track layouts are restricted because sectional track is designed to suit typical or conventional designs. Also, the more joints or connecting points there are in a model track system, the greater the chance of broken or weak electrical connections and a bumpy ride for the train. Flexible track, which you cut yourself to the exact measurements you want, is what the experts recommend.

Flexible track comes in several versions. Some of it is ready-made and needs only to be cut to size. Other forms come with rails, spikes and ties.

Rails are normally made of brass, steel or nickel-silver. The nickel-silver combination requires the least amount of maintenance and provides good traction, but is the least effective material for electrical conductivity. The best conductor is brass, but it is more difficult to solder than the other two metals. Steel is the compromise material.

You can buy ready-made roadbed or make it yourself. You can also buy individual ties and strips of rail as well as the spikes you will need to realistically nail it down. This is an area, however, for the relatively advanced modeler.

Unless you have the simplest of configurations, your track system will require switches and crossings or turnouts. These are available ready-made and are usually a wise purchase in that form: the margin of error in attempting to make these parts yourself is quite large. Many modelers do, however, opt to build their own. There are guidebooks to provide help in this area.

Once track has been laid, it will need to be maintained well if you want to keep your trains running smoothly and efficiently. Rails can pick up dust, lint, stains, smudges and other potential obstacles to good operation. Perhaps the best way to keep rails clean is to periodically wipe them care-

fully with a clean, lint-free, dry cloth. You can use a pencil eraser to remove tougher smudges. Be sure to hold the track down tightly while you wipe it so that you do not break it free of its moorings or twist or bend it by your rubbing action.

There are model railroad track cleaning rigs, or vehicles. Several are sold by Twinn-K. These little machines come with four-wheel drive for added traction, an electrical pickup much like that of a model locomotive, a spring-loaded abrasive pad, a wiping mechanism and a tank to hold cleaning fluid. It runs along the track as a train does, but cleans the rails as it goes. There are other types of track-cleaning machines that can be coupled to a train. They handle the track-maintenance chores while the train operates normally. Use of one of these little machines is certainly a more entertaining way of cleaning track than scouring the rails yourself.

We have seen some very impressive layouts that were made of snap-together sectional track; and we have been dazzled by some extraordinary track systems that were built entirely from scratch, the modeler having fashioned everything by hand, down to staining the wooden ties realistically and spiking each rail to them.

That proves one thing: you can develop an intriguing, authentic-looking layout regardless of your budgetary and artistic limitations. In planning, designing and building a model railroad track, ingenuity is a modelers's greatest asset.

1

2

3

Track should be kept clean to assure that the model train will run smoothly. It can be scrubbed by hand, but there are more entertaining ways to keep track clean. Motorized track-cleaning vehicles are available from several manufacturers. Those from Twinn-K (1,2) are designed to run alone on the tracks. The cleaning machine from Model Die Casting (3) is actually a locomotive. It can pull a line of cars as it cleans the track. Most types of track-cleaning machines use felt or abrasive pads and a solvent to polish the track's rails.

Environments

2

Environmental features are available in scales to match the scales of model trains. Bridges, buildings and trees are made to suit Marklin's very small Mini-Club trains (1). The SEE-NIKS line of environmental products from Associated Hobby Manufacturers includes various landscaping materials and trees in HO scale (2). City scenes surrounding model train layouts often include cars and modern buildings (3).

HAVE YOU EVER wanted to move a mountain, transplant a forest, build a town or tear one down? Such seemingly superhuman feats are well within the power of the model railroader. The design and construction of a model railroad environment—including those mountains, forests and towns—adds a dimension of realism and artistry to a train system.

The track you lay can take your train through a twisting mountain pass, through a tunnel, across a trestle that spans a gorge, past quaint Swiss chalets or through modern American communities. Your train can be made to stop along the way to pick up and unload cargo of all kinds.

Careful planning, a wise selection of mass-produced decorations and some skill in fabricating unique landscape features can result in a model train system that looks astonishingly lifelike. The design of an environment is a personal thing, limited only by your creativity, ambition and budget. An attractive environment can be created, whether you want to put a little or a lot of effort into it.

There are ready-made scale models of many kinds of environmental features, from human figures to apartment buildings. You can buy kits that are simple and inexpensive or complex and costly. Materials, tools and instructional guides are available to those modelers who wish to construct their

3

1

environments from scratch. The choice is up to you.

Some modelers begin with simple kits and gradually add more elaborate ones as they progress in the hobby. Other modelers simply tire of a particular environmental design and rearrange the components to form a new one. You may build an intricate environment that pleases you for the present but will require significant modification later as you complete work on a new part, such as a wooden bridge that you intend to build over a period of months.

Some modelers, in fact, refer to their environmental scenes as "lifetime layouts" because the scenes are projects they will be working on for a lifetime. Some hobbies have beginnings and ends. Model railroading is not one of them. There is no definite end.

There is, however, a beginning. In terms of a model railroad environment, the project begins with planning. Throughout your work on an environmental scene, you will be doing the work of a landscaper, an architect and a city planner. You will need as detailed a plan in designing your model train environment as you needed in developing a layout for the track.

The two — the track and the environment through which it will run — are very much a part of one another. The environment will be restricted by the same space considerations that influence the layout, and the course the train follows will directly affect the types of environmental features you will be able to use.

That is why we noted in the previous chapter the need for a sketch of the layout including the environmental items. This blueprint may help you discover problems in the environment under consideration before you spend a great deal of time and money on a layout. The more complex the environment and layout is to be, the more complete should be the drawings you make of it in the planning stages.

Another step in the planning is a determination of the way you will begin construction. Some modelers lay the track first, then add environmental items little by little; others create a textured terrain and set up their towns before laying any track.

No matter which operation you undertake first, you'll want to have a good idea of the types of products available. By browsing through hobby shops and catalogs from model railroad manufacturers, you will accumulate a lot of information

1

2

Kibri's Make-A-Layout Kit consists of plastic panels covered with simulated grass. Several can be used in combination to form a complete layout (1). The more complex the environmental scene, the greater the need for planning before construction begins (2). For some modelers, the process of building a layout never stops. These "lifetime layouts" continue to grow as new shrubs are added and mountains are enlarged over a period of time (3, 4).

3

1

about the materials you may want to use in creating the scene of your choice.

Terrain and Landscaping

Very often, a modeler's work on a train environment progresses from the ground up, as he fashions the "earth" over which the train will travel. Flat terrain, rolling hills, mountains and valleys can all be created—either before the track is laid or little by little over a period of time while the train remains operational.

Plaster is used to build up the "land." Almost any kind of earth formation can be duplicated in this way. It can be used to make the low-lying features of the terrain and form a foundation for other, more prominent features such as hills and mountains.

Many types of products are available to give the plaster the look of real ground. Colored sawdust can be used to simulate grass; paint can sometimes be used to color the plaster realistically.

Experienced modelers sometimes create their own trees and shrubs by using a variety of materials. This takes time and skill, but it can result in a truly unique and very attractive landscape. It is also possible to use living plants in a model train landscape. Moss, ferns, lichen and various houseplants can be incorporated into a miniature scene. Chosen carefully, such plants can be made to resemble larger forms of vegetation.

For the beginner, however, realistic kits and ready-made trees and shrubs may be the best way to go. A wide variety of them are available, and they all look very realistic. Some of them are made by Peco, Woodland Scenics, SEE—NIKS and Campbell Scale Model.

Some kits contain much more than just the trees and shrubs. These include the vegetation as well as

2

3

"Smiley's Tow Service" is available from Woodland Scenics in HO scale (1). Campbell makes many kits including the wharf kit made of wood (2). SEE-NIKS trees come in many shapes and sizes (3)

rock formations and other features. When completed, they make an entire scene all by themselves. Several of them can be used, perhaps with some modification by the modeler so that they blend in well with one another.

If you want your train to run through the mountains, you can buy a ready-made mountain or a kit, or make a mountain yourself from scratch. Among the kits available are those from Mountains in Minutes, Life-Like Products and MLR. Pre-made models are usually less realistic in appearance than those that are carefully built and finished by hand. But, as far as mountains go, $10 to $20 will get you a fairly large mountain.

Ready-made mountains may not fit your scheme. They can be difficult to alter, so you may have to make other concessions in order to fit one into your layout. A hand-made mountain can be built to fit a specific design, but building your own mountain or

mountain range takes time and know-how. Yet this is not beyond the capabilities of many modelers.

If you decide to build a replica mountain, there are several steps to follow that will help to ensure a finished model that will please you.

The first step is to design and mold the basic shape. Plan well what you want the mountain to look like, studying photographs and making sketches. Foothills, caves, deep gorges, chasms and various other outcroppings must be planned for before you actually begin construction.

The best way to define the shape of a model mountain is uncomplicated and about as inexpensive as possible. Many modelers wad up old newspapers or paper towels around a simple support structure made of wood. You can use masking tape to hold the paper in place. Spraying the paper with water from a plant sprayer will also help to hold it in place.

You shape your mountain by hand as you go along. Once you have the contours of your mountain defined with the wadded-up paper, you are ready to apply an outer covering. You can do this with strips of heavy-duty paper towels dipped in a thin plaster solution. You can find inexpensive molding plaster at almost any lumber or building supply store. The strips of paper should be about one or two inches wide and six inches to a foot long. Saturate the paper towel strip in the liquid plaster, and then lay it on top of the paper wads. As you lay each strip in place, keep in mind that the plaster-coated paper should not only give you the shape you desire for your mountain, but also should make the mountain strong. A thickness of one-quarter inch is ideal, but you can get by with less than that.

If you want to make a tunnel through the mountain as most modelers do, you can plan for it before plastering, or cut it out of the mountain afterwards. Most experienced modelers we talked to said that the latter approach is best.

If you attack the tunnel after building the mountain structure, all you do is cut out a section of plaster; remove the newspaper from inside the mountain; insert a support for the roadbed and track if one is needed; and then fashion the tunnel entrance and exit portals. Tunnel portals, already made to suit most applications, are available in a large variety of styles and types at hobby shops.

Once you have structured the mountain, the next job is to make it look realistic. To achieve a rocklike texture, you can brush on additional coats of plaster or liquid latex with a paint brush. You can also buy mixtures of rocklike materials to put on your mountain. To approximate the true color of mountainous rock—the grays, tans and rusts—many experienced modelers advise against using paint. Instead, they recommend solutions of clothing dyes that you have mixed to the desired color. These can be applied with brushes, cotton balls and sponges. The plaster accepts the colors readily.

From this point on, what you make your mountain look like is a tribute to your artistry and craftsmanship. It is a help to study pictures of mountains for various features and then try to re-create some of these, either from scratch or by using some of the scale model trees, shrubs and other products available.

Rivers, Lakes and Bridges

The visual drama of a model railroad system can be heightened greatly by skillfully designed bodies of water. The water, of course, is not real, but something made to look like real water. Therein lies the artistry.

Railroads in real life often follow the shoreline of rivers and lakes, crisscrossing them where necessary on bridges of all types. Railroads often link up with canals and run to the edges of oceans. That is why the look of such bodies of water lends an appearance of authenticity to a model railroad.

Real water would leak, become stagnant, and could even present a safety hazard when used in an electric model railroad system. There are some problems to overcome in using artificial water in a system also. The fact is that there are no synthetic ponds, rivers, streams or lakes available in ready-made or kit form. Model railroaders who want to incorporate bodies of water into their layouts must fashion them from scratch. But the task is not a difficult one and the results can be strikingly realistic.

The first step is to cut out or form the bed or channel of the river or lake. It does not have to be deep, because you will not be filling it with much of anything, but it should look realistic. That will require some sculpting of shorelines and banks. You can gouge out areas that must be deepened and you can shore up other areas with plaster, putty or other fillers.

There are various materials that can be used to simulate water. Glass, cellophane and clear plastic can be cut to shape, but such materials tend to look more like ice than water. Mottled clear plastic or opaque glass will give another impression, but not one that is always very realistic. You can touch up the surfaces by brushing on varnish, clear glue, or other material that will give the surface the appearance of moving water.

Many modelers, however, prefer to construct their water areas from clear casting resin. This liquid plastic is generally available at hobby shops, hardware stores and sometimes art supply outlets. This method involves pouring the liquid casting resin into the water area. The resin will solidify. As it does, you can shape it and sculpt it to resemble waves.

To cross such bodies of water, ravines between mountains and other would-be obstacles, a train needs a bridge. Full-size bridges are made of huge wooden beams or concrete steel girders. The model railroader can duplicate these bridges in miniature in a variety of ways.

In the world of model railroading, bridges can be among the most visually exciting features of a layout. Many sophisticated systems are built around an intricate bridge so that all the observer's attention is focused on the train's progress high above the layout platform.

There are double-track and single-track bridges, trestle bridges and truss bridges, causeways and covered bridges. Many of these are available in kits at hobby shops, in scales to match that of the rest of the train layout. Others are ready to be used just as they come from their packages.

However, a part of the hobby of model railroading that can provide many hours of enjoyment for an experienced craftsman is the construction of a detailed replica bridge from scratch. These bridges are feats of engineering as well as craftsmanship.

1

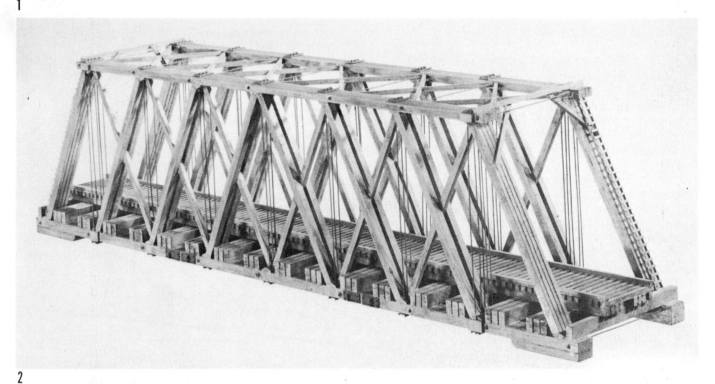

2

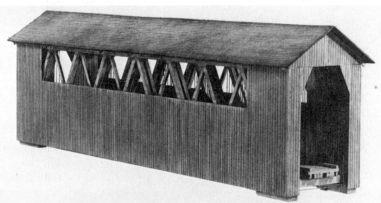

Bridges allowing the model train to cross over rivers and gorges are very often the most dramatic features of a layout. Several types of bridges are available from Campbell Scale Models in kit form. The bridges--the Howe Truss (1), the covered bridge (2) and the tall trestle (3)--are made of wood. Assembly is just one step in the use of such a kit; weathering to create the look of a real bridge is an art in itself.

3

Buildings and City Scenes

The assortment of buildings available to the model railroader seems unlimited. There are simple kits and extremely complex kits of nearly every kind of structure from little bungalows to big skyscrapers. There are houses, stores, railroad stations and other types of buildings from the era of the first Iron Horse up to the present. The range of what you can create is vast.

You can design and lay out an entire town, building each and every structure with your own hands. If your Wild West town is to have a saloon, you build it and put it where you want. If you want a delicately detailed Victorian house in your turn-of-the-century city, you will have a broad array of kits to choose from. In a large hobby shop, you'll find everything from a sheriff's office to a factory; from a miner's shack to a one-piece Main Street.

When you make your layout blueprint, you should determine what period in railroad history you want to re-create. Then you will have to determine how many pieces you can put into the scene and what your personal priorities are in terms of individual buildings or structures. And you will have to determine just how much of a hand you will want in the construction of each item.

Many scale model buildings are available completely assembled or nearly so. They require little work on the part of the model railroader.

If you decide to buy kits, you will find a wide variety of products to choose from. There are simple beginners' kits that simply snap together. Many are prepainted or molded in color. On the other hand, there are many sophisticated kits that require the skills of an experienced modeler. Among the scale structures available in kit form are the extremely handsome and well-detailed ones from Magnuson Models and Vollmer, two of the most respected names in this branch of the model railroading hobby. Other fine products are marketed by Kibri, Suydam, Scale Structures, and Classic Miniatures, Atlas and Campbell. Kits contain detailed, step-by-step instructions, but you will no doubt develop some of your own techniques as you go along, especially in the areas of painting and detailing.

The time and effort spent by some modelers on the construction and finishing of these structures is remarkable. To give a replica building the look of having gone through perhaps hundreds of years of exposure to the elements, modelers sometimes spend countless hours in painting it. The use of many different types of paint on a single building is a painstaking and time-consuming process, but it can result in weathering that is surprisingly close in appearance to full-size buildings. In fact, some photographs of these scale model buildings can easily be mistaken for photos of real-life structures.

Unless you are interested only in ghost towns or purely scenes of nature, you will surely want to put some life into the environmental scene. Old towns in the West had cowboys, horses, wagons and stagecoaches, hitching posts and water troughs. Newer towns have cars, buses, stoplights, fire hydrants, traffic signs, paved streets, garbage cans, fences and sidewalks. In the country, farms have farmers, cows, ducks, chickens, pigs—the whole

Another model from Campbell is the Wild West Saloon, suitable for use with replicas of 1890s trains.

Careful planning and skill in weathering result in miniature scenes that look astoundingly real.

menagerie. They also have tractors, windmills, and so on.

There are all kinds of figures, vehicles and other items of city and country scenes available. Some are made of metal; others of plastic. Some are already assembled and painted; others you will have to paint and finish yourself. Companies offering human and animal figures include Merten, Preiser, Kibri, Weston and Scale Structures.

As an example of the importance of careful detailing in the hobby, consider the planning done by fanciers of model traction equipment.

The environment for traction equipment varies with the specific type of train or trolley you choose. Interurban trains travel through the same scenery that regular model railroads do, but they may also run on city street tracks and elevated tracks. Interurban trains, at least in the open country, follow the same kind of broad, sweeping curves as long-distance trains; but in the city where they would travel slower, the interurbans would be able to negotiate tighter turns than an ordinary steam or diesel train.

Model trolleys or streetcars would be found only in an urban environment, traveling the streets, handling sharp turns. A traction setup of this nature is ideal for modelers who are hampered by limited space.

City environments for traction equipment are generally more elaborate in terms of structures and street designs than are urban settings for non-traction trains. There are, in fact, specific structures and accessories available for traction

scenes—specialized car barns, or elevated structures and terminals.

Mechanical Equipment

Real trains are loaded with cargo at one location and are unloaded at their destinations. Real trains pass under drawbridges that close as the cabooses flash by. As real trains approach streets, the thoroughfares are blocked from automobile traffic by crossing gates.

All of these operations are possible with model trains also. Realism and action, even a bit of humor, can be added to a model railroad system through the use of a variety of mechanical accessories. Some of these devices are operated manually by the railroader; some go into operation automatically each time the train runs over a particular section of track; others are operated by remote control from the power pack's control panel.

There are loading and unloading mechanisms, crossing gates and many other accessories. Some of them are designed not for realism but for amusement. As an example, Bachmann markets a device called "The Cowardly Cow and the Frantic Farmer" which rescues Bossie from an oncoming train. A Bachman train set called "The Great Iron Horse Train Robbery" includes a trap-door car, an "exploding" car, a miniature robber who dangles from a trestle and other moving parts that enable model railroaders to reenact the entire drama.

There is no end to the kinds of environmental accessories that a model railroader can add to a system over a period of time.

Power Packs and Wiring

1

MODEL RAILROADS, with only rare exception today, are powered by electricity. The basic design of their electrical systems is simple. Even those whose experience with electricity has not gone beyond turning lights on and off and occasionally plugging in an electrical appliance can, with a little help and guidance, easily master the basics of getting a model train to move smoothly over a track energized by electricity from an ordinary household outlet.

As model railroading grows in complexity, however—when switches and other electrically operated equipment are added, another train is in-troduced, the track is lengthened, or grades are increased—the requirements of the electrical system will also become much greater. As a person moves ahead in the hobby of model railroading, knowledge and experience will also grow and in most cases will compensate for the new requirements in electrical work and wiring. And even then, the entire task will still be relatively uncomplicated.

There are guidebooks that thoroughly cover all aspects of model railroad wiring, put out by publishers like Kalmbach Books and Carstens Publications and model manufacturers such as Atlas Tool Company. With help from these publications you

2

The variety of power packs used with model trains is almost as great as the variety of trains themselves. One power pack made by Model Rectifier Corp. is the Throttlepack 501 (1). It is capable of powering up to five HO trains or seven N scale trains. Troller Corp. makes many different power packs in a wide range of prices and power ratings (2). MRC makes several simple power packs including the Trainpack (3) and the Railine 300 (4), designed for hobbyists who want to make their first step up from the power packs that come packaged with train sets. All power packs, whether they are simple or complex, perform the same electrical function: they transform household AC to direct current, making the electricity safe to use even by very young children.

3

4

can ordinarily handle the most difficult electrical problems of advanced modeling. Until your model railroad reaches a high level of sophistication, you needn't fret over this aspect of model railroading. You can easily get by with a knowledge of just the basics, which we provide in this chapter. The information here and the instructional guidelines that come with a power pack will prepare you well for the operation of your train. In fact, for most basic layouts, the electrical work is not really much more than simply hooking the wires from the power pack to the track, plugging the power pack into a wall outlet and then operating the controls.

It is a good idea, however, to know just what is going on in your model's electrical system. You will probably become more involved in this aspect of the hobby later; and you may have to make repairs, adjustments or modifications of your setup at the beginning.

Household current, called alternating current or simply AC, is too powerful for use with a miniature railroad. Therefore, it must be transformed into direct current, or DC, at a much lower voltage.

A model railroad power pack, once called simply a transformer, is what converts normal incoming AC current to current that is safe and effective for

Tyco's System 200 train set comes complete with two trains and two power packs that allow the trains to be operated separately. As the sets grow additional power may be needed.

your purposes in model railroading. In the power pack, the 110-volt AC current is actually transformed into two types of current: 12-volt DC to power the model locomotive; and 16-volt AC for operating accessories like switches, lighting equipment and other auxiliary apparatus.

DC current, unlike alternating current, flows only in one direction until it is reversed. To power the train, therefore, the current must be passed to the locomotive and then returned to the power pack. One wire carries the electrical energy to the right-hand rail of the track. The locomotive's engine picks up the current from this track and returns it by way of the left-hand track through a second wire leading back to the power pack. Clear, brief instructions for hooking the power pack's wire to the track come with the power packs.

The reason why accessories are not powered by the same DC current is that they would place too much of a strain on the single 12-volt DC capacity. When in operation, they would drain off energy from the locomotive, which would slow down and operate roughly. But with the capability of dual currents found in good power packs, you will have a system that functions without faltering when increased power is called for. But remember this very important point: Be sure that the power wires for the locomotive are hooked to the DC terminals of

the power pack; if you inadvertently hook the rail wires to the AC terminal, you could burn out your locomotive.

Keep in mind that what we are talking about here is basic wiring for a simple oval layout and a single train. If you decide you want another train to run concurrently with the first, or you redesign your track to include such things as loops, wyes (a switch where tracks curve away in opposite directions), and return cutoffs—the kind of equipment that requires remote-control switches—you will have to adjust your electrical system accordingly. This is where the electrical wiring can become a bit more difficult and this is where you will have to seek guidance in books providing in-depth coverage of the subject, or from a highly experienced model railroader.

You can run two engines on one oval track at the same time with a single power pack and a single set of wires if the power pack is strong enough. The trains, of course, will run only at the same time and at the same speed, and will stop simultaneously because their power comes from the same source.

A means of running two trains independently on the same track is called gapping. This requires separate track sections, usually called blocks, to be made by cutting gaps in the track. That is, you cut the rail so that the flow of current is broken to that area of track; then a separate hookup is made so that a train running in one block will operate independently of the train moving in the other block. This way, one train can be brought to a halt while the other is still moving, for example, or the two can be operated at slightly different speeds. Control is from a push-button or toggle switch that has been incorporated into the power pack's control panel. You can also achieve a gapping effect by using insulated (plastic) rail joiners.

There are other methods of operating complex model railroad systems. For these and for gapping, however, we advise study of the subject. Seek the help of a skilled model railroader because this is an intricate operation.

The Power Pack

The core of any model railroader's electrical system is the power pack. By definition it is a transformer and rectifier that converts 110-volt AC current into 12-volt DC current, with the capabilities to control train speed, braking and direction.

One of the problems novice model railroaders often encounter is that the power pack they acquire is not powerful enough for their purposes. Power packs that come with train sets, for example, are invariably just powerful enough to move the locomotive and three or four cars around a small oval track. If you were to add track, additional railroad cars or other electrical accessories, the power pack would not be able to handle the load.

On the other hand, if you don't start with a set but choose to put together the individual pieces of the model railroad system yourself, it is still possible to purchase a power pack that is not strong enough for your needs or one that the rest of your system will outgrow. Price enters the picture here. Power packs vary considerably in cost, from as little as $20 up to $200. In an effort to save money, you may underestimate what will serve your purposes.

Railroad operators must be able to judge how heavy a load can be pulled by a particular locomotive. Sometimes two or more locomotives are coupled together to pull extremely heavy cargo or very long chains of cars. The situation is similar in model railroading. Power requirements are important when the modeler makes a decision to buy a certain locomotive. Nearly all of the model locomotives used today are powered by electricity (some use clockwork-type mechanisms or steam power, but they are very rare). They differ in how much electricity they can use and how well they use it.

The efficiency of the locomotive is important in setting up and operating a model train system, and so is the power available from a particular power pack. The strength of the current produced by a power pack is measured in amperes, or amps, and this rating is usually printed on the face of the control panel. The following chart gives the basic acceptable amperage for the three most common

1

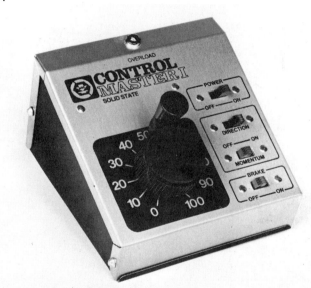

2

The Railine 370 (1) and the Control Master I (2), also from Model Rectifier Corp., provide more features than do the simplest power packs. Realistic acceleration and braking are two of the features of the Control Master.

scale model railroads. The requirements apply to the operation of a single train.

Scale	Ampere Rating
N	1/2 to 1
HO	1 to 2
O	2 to 4

Of course, the locomotives used with power packs influence how well the system will operate. The weight of the locomotive is important. A locomotive and power pack may be powerful enough to pull many cars, but the locomotive may be so

A look under the body of an N scale locomotive from Atlas Tool Co. shows how the motor is designed. The motor--the light-colored cylinder--drives eight of the locomotive's wheels. The Atlas locomotives in N scale and HO scale have flywheels attached to their motors. The company says the flywheel helps to ensure smooth operation.

light that its drive wheels slip on the rails. A heavier engine with the same power would have better traction and probably would be able to pull the train more effectively. If the locomotive is too heavy, however, it could require more power to get under way than the power pack can provide. The relationship between the locomotive and the power pack is important to remember when shopping for either component, separately or together.

There are a number of different power packs to choose from in today's hobby marketplace. Such respected names in the industry as Marnold, Model Rectifier Corporation, Autopulse H and M, and Pacific Fast Mail, to name only a few, offer a variety of excellent power packs.

They are similar to one another in several ways. Power packs have throttle controls that utilize either a rheostat or a transistorized throttle. A rheostat is an adjustable resistor that allows a desired amount of current to pass through itself to the track. Transistorized throttles work in a similar way, but offer a greater degree of control over the locomotive than rheostats do, and therefore provide a more uniform ride either at steady speeds or during acceleration and deceleration. Rheostats, however, are nevertheless preferred by some advanced modelers, especially because of the savings

in cost: transistor units can cost much more than rheostat throttles.

Some power packs are designed so that you can operate more than one train at a time. Several power packs, each with controls for only one train, can be used simultaneously in a control panel. Such a panel can also be used to house the various switches and controls for other apparatus built into an elaborate system.

When selecting a power pack, it is wise to consider your immediate objectives, while also taking into consideration your long-range plans.

Your local hobby shop owner or operator probably will be happy to discuss your present setup or plans for a set-up. Let him know what your future plans are, and he may be able to recommend a power pack that will be right for you in the immediate and distant future.

Problem Solving

Model railroaders, beginners and experts alike, occasionally have power problems with their track systems. These problems are inevitable, considering how many separate electrical connections make up a model railroad track. Here are some symptoms of electrical faults:

The train moves erratically, stopping and starting again all by itself.

The train loses power on certain sections of the track, laboring when it should be running smoothly.

The train moves more swiftly on straight, level sections of the track than it does on turns or grades.

The train slows down as it moves to the most distant portions of the track.

The locomotive hums but does not move.

The train does not move or hum; nothing seems to be working.

The latter problem could be something as simple as a disconnected wall plug. The cause of other problems may take a little more work to find, but solving these problems can be almost as simple as reinserting a plug. A simple checklist can help you isolate the difficulty.

● Examine the wires from the power pack to the track to make certain that they are connected properly.

● Check the fit of the locomotive's wheels on the rails. The wheels should roll smoothly while on the track.

● Inspect the locomotive for any loose or detached wires.

● Check the locomotive for obstructions that would prevent its wheels from turning smoothly. It could need cleaning or lubrication.

● Disconnect several cars from the train, or run the locomotive by itself. The load on the engine may be too heavy.

● Look at the track carefully to see whether it needs cleaning. A dirty track cannot adequately transmit electricity to the locomotive.

● Check the connections at each track segment to make sure that all of them are tight.

● If possible, lower any inclined areas of the track to see whether the problem is caused by grades that are too steep for the locomotive to climb.

● If possible, shorten the track. The problems may result from track that is too long to be adequately energized by the power pack.

If, after you have checked all of these areas, the train system still malfunctions, you may have to consult hobby shop personnel. However, unless the inner workings of the power pack or the locomotive have been damaged, most problems in the operation of a model railroad can be solved at home, and you won't need the skills of Thomas Edison to do it yourself.

A note about traction train systems: The power for model traction equipment, replicas of trains that get their electrical power from overhead cables, can be transmitted to the model trains in two ways. The first way, the more complicated of the two, uses energized wires positioned over the track in much the same manner as the full-size traction systems do. Equipment of this kind is readily available, and there are several good books on the subject. The easier method is to use electrical tracks such as those used for non-traction train systems. When this technique is used, model railroaders often string "dummy" wires above the track to give the system a look of authenticity.

Some replicas of traction trolleys and trains can be powered by electric current passed through the rails. Others, however, like those from LGB, get their electrical power from wires over the track.

Sources

Associations & Organizations

SOME HOBBIES have several national organizations to represent the interests of serious modelers. Model railroading has only one major national group, the National Model Railroad Association, which is described below. There are, however, thousands of model railroad clubs in North America, located in all but the most remote geographic areas. The clubs, which may or may not be affiliated with NMRA, generally offer a variety of services, events, get-togethers, competitions, forums for the exchange of ideas, and perhaps even markets for the trade or sale of equipment. The person who owns or manages the hobby shop in your area can usually direct you to the club or clubs that are operating near you.

National Model Railroad Association (NMRA)
P.O. Box 2186
Indianapolis, IN 46206

The major organization in model railroading is

the NMRA, which was founded back in 1935 in Milwaukee, Wisconsin, and has been run for the sake of several generations of model railroaders ever since. Today, the NMRA has almost 30,000 members in 14 regions covering the United States and Canada, and one region for Great Britain.

Benefits of NMRA membership are many. The *NMRA Bulletin,* an informative magazine, is published each month and sent free of charge to all members. Also published by the NMRA is a *Directory of Information* that details the association's administrative setup, committees, by-laws and contest rules; presents an official glossary of model railroading terms; and contains the complete text of the NMRA Standards and Recommended Practices. NMRA standards were developed back in the early days of the organization and now serve as a guide for hobbyists as well as the model railroad industry. This is something you will want to have if you are really serious about the hobby. Also, the

NMRA publishes an annual index of the articles in all major model railroading publications.

The *Data-Pack* is a book the NMRA offers as an option. It contains a vast amount of information for truly serious railroad modelers including technical data about full-size prototype railroads and recommendations on how to render all the details in scale models. It is highly regarded by the experts in model railroading. It will cost you an additional $10 when you order it from the NMRA.

Among the organization's other offerings are tape and slide programs covering a wide range of railroading subjects. They can be rented inexpensively. The association also sponsors a nationally recognized achievement program, and holds a national convention each year in July or August (the location rotates through seven major geographical areas of the United States).

All the benefits of NMRA membership cost $10 a year. Special rates for families are available.

Publications

Periodicals

THE HOBBY OF model railroading is fortunate to have a wide range of magazines and periodicals that cover areas of general interest as well as various specialized forms of modeling and collecting. These publications provide a forum for the exchange of ideas as well as a medium for interesting, in-depth articles on the various arts and crafts of railroad modeling. Most are richly illustrated. And they are timely, keeping the serious modeler abreast of what is going on in the model railroad world — everything from the presentation of new techniques to the announcement of competitions, exhibitions and other noteworthy events, plus evaluations of new products.

Locomotive Quarterly, P.O. Box 288, Homewood, IL 60430. A slick, handsome publication, *Locomotive Quarterly* is devoted to preserving the color, romance and nostalgia of steam railroading. The graphics are first-rate: this is a publication that you will probably not discard once you have looked through it. The quarterly is as valuable for the information it offers as it is for the quality of its illustrations. It is available by subscription. Back issues can be ordered.

Model Railroader, Kalmbach Publishing Co., 1027 N. 7th St., Milwaukee, WI 53233. This is perhaps the premier publication in the field of model railroading: it has been serving the railroad hobbyist for more than 40 years. Wide-ranging articles — as many as eight or 10 per issue — informative and timely departments, idea-trading, product reviews

and the greatest amount of advertising of products offered by any publication in the field are what this magazine has to offer to the model railroad enthusiast. Information can be as fundamental as what to look for in buying a simple train set or as ambitious as instructions for building a turntable from scratch. There is something here for all levels of modelers, whether you are just starting out or have become a seasoned pro after years of effort. The magazine also contains up-to-date listings of model railroad retailers and hobby shops by state. Published monthly, it is available by subscription and at newsstands and hobby shops. Back issues are available.

Narrow Gauge & Short Line Gazette, Gazette Publications, 800 San Antonio Rd., Palo Alto, CA 94302. For the aficionado of narrow-gauge modeling, this is an interesting and handsome publication that

provides a wide range of informative articles and pleasing graphics. The *Narrow Gauge & Short Line Gazette* is a magazine that covers model building as well as the world of full-size trains. Available by subscription and at some hobby shops.

NMRA Bulletin, National Model Railroad Association, P.O. Box 2186, Indianapolis, IN 46202. The official publication of the National Model Railroad Association, the *Bulletin* provides page after page of railroad modeling information as well as news of past, present and future events and activities of the association. Once a year, the *Bulletin* includes a periodical index that catalogs the articles that have appeared in all major model railroad magazines during the previous 12 months. This can be a valuable feature for any serious modelers. The *NMRA Bulletin* is a monthly publication that is included as part of NMRA membership.

Passenger Train Journal, P.O. Box 397, Park Forest, IL 60466. Like *Trains,* the periodical *Passenger Train Journal* is about the real world of railroading rather than the hobby world of model trains. But it is a fine source for the modeler interested in passenger trains and the newest equipment, trends and innovations in this field. It can also provide many ideas for the creative modeler to later render in scale. Highly illustrated, it is as appropriate for the modeling enthusiast as it is for the train buff. Published monthly, available by subscription.

Prototype Modeler, 171½ Pine St., P.O. Box 343, Danvers, MA 01923. This magazine—in its present format—is a newcomer to the model railroad scene. The parent company has for years published materials specifically on the railroads that ran the tracks west of the Mississippi River; now the new magazine takes on all the railroads of the United States. It is a useful and interesting source for those interested in prototype modeling. It is published monthly and is available by subscription.

Rail Classics, Challenge Publications Inc., 7950 Deering Ave., Canoga Park, CA 91304. This is another periodical directed to train enthusiasts, whether or not they are modelers. Well-written, well-illustrated articles about the real world of railroading contained in each issue will be of interest to all modelers. This magazine also includes a full-color section with good photographs in each issue. It is published six times a year and can be obtained by subscription or at newsstands.

Railfan, Carstens Publications Inc., P.O. Box 700, Newton, NJ 07860. *Railfan* is one of the two major periodicals to come from Carstens Publications, long a respected publisher of model railroad books and periodicals. (The other is *Railroad Model Craftsman.*) *Railfan* focuses on full-size railroads. Good, solid articles and informative departmental

offerings will, however, appeal to advanced modelers. The articles are broad in scope, authoritative in their presentation, and well illustrated. Railroad news, views and events and some model-related advertising are also part of this magazine. *Railfan* is for all fans of railroads. Published bimonthly, it is available by subscription and at many newsstands.

Railroad Model Craftsman, Carstens Publications Inc., P.O. Box 700, Newton, NJ 07860. One of the major magazines in the field of model railroading, *Railroad Model Craftsman* is a good source of information, tips and ideas. Articles by experts cover many areas of modeling and collecting. Departmental features keep readers up-to-date on news and happenings in the model railroad world. New products are tested, evaluated and reviewed in each issue. There is a good amount of product advertising and a large and helpful classified ad section for trading. It is an informative and well-illustrated publication that will benefit beginners as well as advanced modelers. *Railroad Model Craftsman* contains a comprehensive state-by-state listing of hobby shops that cater to model railroaders. Published monthly; available by subscription, at newsstands and at many hobby shops.

Railroad Modeler, Challenge Publications Inc., 7950 Deering Ave., Canoga Park, CA 91304 This is the principal railroad modeling magazine from Challenge Publications, one of the largest publishers of periodicals in the hobby field—*Scale Modeler, Military Modeler* and others. *Railroad Modeler* is directed toward modelers of varying levels of skill and experience. It contains a wide variety of lively and informative articles. Product critiques are an important part of this publication; they consist of in-depth reviews with precise evaluations. Book reviews, current news and announcements, and tips on new modeling techniques and innovations are other features of this monthly magazine. Available by subscription or at many newsstands and hobby stores.

Railway Quarterly, Challenge Publications Inc., 7950 Deering Ave., Canoga Park, CA 91304. *Railway Quarterly* is a new entry: its first issue was published in the fall of 1977. It is also a new concept and is noticeably different from any other publication on the market today. Each issue focuses on one particular theme of railroading and stays with that subject. A recent issue, for example, offered an in-depth look at "The Passenger Scene." A variety of articles on a single theme as well as other related information provide fresh and thorough insights for both the train buff and the railroad modeler. This illustrated quarterly is available by subscription and at newsstands.

S. Gauge Herald, P.O. Box 105, Oradell, NJ 07649. This is a specialty publication, the most direct and comprehensive source of information on S scale (1:64 scale) railroad modeling. The magazine has tips for the beginner as well as detailed articles on custom building for the expert. Product evaluations are highlighted; and news of events, present and future, for S scale modelers is included. The *Herald* is fully illustrated and is very reasonably priced. Available by subscription or at hobby shops.

Traction & Models Magazine, 6710 Hampton Drive East, Indianapolis, IN 46226. Hailed as the "100% traction monthly," this magazine offers interesting and informative articles on this area of modeling (street cars, interurbans, heavy electrics, etc.). Model building tips and techniques, book and product reviews, diagrams, plans and a classified ad section contribute to the value of this publication. Published monthly, it is available by subscription or at hobby shops.

Trains, Kalmbach Publishing Co., 1027 N. 7th St., Milwaukee, WI 53233. This highly illustrated magazine offers something for all train lovers. It is about railroads and those things closely associated with them in the real world, but the publication caters to the modeler's interests as well. From nostalgic history to the newest innovations, from the iron horse to Amtrak, *Trains* presents articles about all aspects of the railroad industry. Current news, book reviews, substantial product advertisement (much of it of interest to the modeler), and an expansive classified ad section are some of the magazine's other features. A monthly publication, *Trains* is available by subscription or at newsstands.

Books

The popularity of model railroading can be judged by the enormous number of books and booklets on the subject that are currently on the market or on library shelves. General books that look at all phases of the hobby as well as highly specialized books on specific technical aspects are available. They can answer almost any question that might arise about model railroading and guide modelers at every level of competence and experience.

There are a number of publishers and other companies that specialize in model railroading books as well as books about full-size trains and railroading. Most provide catalogs or listings of their publications, which can be obtained by writing directly to the companies. The following are the major producers of books specially geared to the interests of the model railroader.

Atlas Railroad Books
Atlas Tool Co. Inc.
378 Florence Ave.
Hillside, NJ 07205

Carstens Publications Inc.
P.O. Drawer 700
Newton, NJ 07860

Glenwood Publishers
P.O. Box 880
Felton, CA 95018

Golden West Books
P.O. Box 8136
San Marino, CA 91108

Kalmbach Books
1027 N. 7th St.
Milwaukee, WI 53233

Kemtron Corp.
P.O. Box 360
Walnut, CA 91789

Ladd Publications Inc.
P.O. Box 137
Jacksonville, IL 62651

Newton K. Gregg
P.O. Box 1459
Rohnert Park, CA 94928

Old Line Publishers
P.O. Box 123
Milwaukee, WI 53201

Profile Publications
979 Third Ave., No. 1703
New York, N.Y. 10017

Prototype Modeler Inc.
171½ Pine St.
P.O. Box 343
Danvers, MA 01923

Walthers Inc.
5601 W. Florist Ave.
Milwaukee, WI 53218

Distributors & Manufacturers

THE FIRST SOURCE for model trains and the many accessories, tools, materials and electronic equipment that go along with them is the local hobby store. There you will find items for inspection and comparison, and in many cases you will be able to profit from the knowledge and experience of shop personnel. Catalogs are also available, usually offering a full assortment of models and related items.

The following is a list of the major manufacturers and distributors of products to serve all the needs of the model railroader. The products available on the market today are many, and provide the beginner as well as the experienced modeler and collector with a large choice of trains and related equipment. Many of the companies listed here provide catalogs (although many charge for them, 25 cents to as much as $4), which detail all their products. Some of the larger firms provide how-to books as well as other publications or services.

TRAIN SETS

Aristo-Polk's International
314 Fifth Ave.
New York, NY 10001

Associated Hobby Manufacturers, Inc.
401 E. Tioga St.
Philadelphia, PA 19134

Bachmann Bros. Inc.
1400 Erie Ave.
Philadelphia, PA 19124

Boyd Models
1835 Whittier Ave.
Building B-1
Costa Mesa, CA 92627

Charmerz Trains
(See Merzbach)

Jouef
(See Aristo-Polk's International)

Life-Like Products, Inc.
1600 Union Ave.
Baltimore, MD 21211

Lionel (Fundimensions)
Div. General Mills Fun Group
Mount Clemens, MI 48045

Marklin
(See Boyd Models and/or Reeves International)

Merzbach Co., Inc.
200 Fifth Ave.
New York, NY 10010

Reeves International
1107 Broadway
New York, NY 10010

Tyco Industries Inc.
540 Glen Ave.
Moorestown, NJ 08057

LOCOMOTIVES AND CARS

Alco Models
P.O. Box 211
Port Jefferson, NY 11777

Ambroid Co. Inc.
P.O. Box 1089
Taunton, MA 02780

American Standard Car Co.
98 Railroad Ave.
Crystal Lake, IL 60014

Arbour Models
P.O. Box 1352
Syracuse, NY 13201

Aristo-Polk's International
314 Fifth Ave.
New York, NY 10001

Associated Hobby Manufacturers
401 E. Tioga St.
Philadelphia, PA 19134

Athearn, Inc.
1510 W. 135th St.
Gardena, CA 90249

Atlas Tool Co. Inc.
378 Florence Ave.
Hillside, NJ 07205

Bachmann Bros. Inc.
1400 Erie Ave.
Philadelphia, PA 19124

Bowser Manufacturing Co.
21 Howard St.
Montoursville, PA 17754

Boyd Models
1835 Whittier Ave.
Building B-1
Costa Mesa, CA 92627

Camino Scale Models
P.O. Box 10666
Eugene, OR 97401

Cary Locomotive Works
308 Three Oaks Rd.
Cary, IL 60013

Central Locomotive Works
2705 Honey Road
Lake Park, FL 33403

Charmerz Trains
(See Merzbach)

Con-Cor
(See JMC International)

Custom Brass
(See N.J. International)

Durango Press
P.O. Box 512
Manhattan Beach, CA 90266

Grandt Line Products
2709 Las Armes
Oakland, CA 94611

Hallmark Models Inc.
4822 Bryan St.
Dallas, TX 75204

Hobby Marketing Inc.
Bldg. 4–96-C Commerce Way
Woburn, MA 01801

Holgate & Reynolds
601 Davis St.
Evanston, IL 60201

JMC International
1025 Industrial Drive
Bensenville, IL 60106

Kadee Quality Products Co.
720 S. Grape St.
Medford, OR 97501

Kemtron Corp.
P.O. Box 360
Walnut, CA 91789

Key Imports Inc.
12 Tara Hill Rd.
Tiburon, CA 94920

Keystone Locomotive Works
159 Wheatley Ave.
Northumberland, PA 17857

Lambert Associates
P.O. Box 4338
San Leandro, CA 94579

L.G.B. National Sales Office
P.O. Box 1247
Milwaukee, WI 53201

Life-Like Products, Inc.
1600 Union Ave.
Baltimore, MD 21211

Locomotive Co.
P.O. Box 1624
Manhattan Beach, CA 90266

Mantua Metal Products Co., Inc.
Grandview Ave.
Woodbury Heights, NJ 08097

Marklin
(See Boyd Models and/or
Reeves International)

G.F. Menzies Co.
P.O. Box 153
Silverton, OR 97381

Merzbach Co. Inc.
200 Fifth Ave.
New York, NY 10010

Midwest Products Co. Inc.
400 S. Indiana St.

Hobart, IN 46342

Model Die Casting Inc.
3811 W. Rosecrans Ave.
Hawthorne, CA 90250

Model Power
180 Smith St.
Farmingdale, NY 11735

Nickel Plate Products
P.O. Box 288
Homewood, IL 60430

N.J. International
22 W. Nicholi St.
Hicksville, NY 11801

Northwest Short Lines
P.O. Box 423
Seattle, WA 98111

Otaki
(See Scale Craft)

Overland Models, Inc.
4001 N. St. Joseph Ave.
Evansville, IN 47712

Pacific Fast Mail
P.O. Box 57
Edmonds, WA 98020

Peco
(See Hobby Marketing)

Quality Craft Models, Inc.
177 Wheatley Ave.
Northumberland, PA 17857

Rapido
(See Stevens International)

Reeves International
1107 Broadway
New York, NY 10010

Rio Grande Models Ltd.
P.O. Box 364
Santa Clara, CA 95054

Roller Bearing Models
P.O. Box 573
Livingston, NJ 07039

Roundhouse Products
(See Model Die Casting)

Scale Craft Models
8735 Shirley Ave.
Northridge, CA 91324

Soho & Co.
P.O. Box 57100
Los Angeles, CA 90057

Stevens International
P.O. Box 2908
Cherry Hill, NJ 08034

Sunset Models
19986 Mallory Ct.
Saratoga, CA 95070

Train-Miniature Products
8140 Center St.
La Mesa, CA 92041

Tyco Industries Inc.
540 Glen Ave.
Moorestown, NJ 08057

Wabash Valley Lines, Inc.
R.R. 2, Sycamore Hollow
Huntington, IN 46750

Wm. K. Walthers Inc.
5601 W. Florist Ave.
Milwaukee, WI 53218

Westside Model Co.
3085 Carriker Lane
Soquel, CA 95073

Williams Reproductions Ltd.
7925 Hammond Pkwy.
Laurel, MD 20810

TRACK SYSTEMS

Alexander Scale Models
P.O. Box 7121
Grand Rapids, MI 49510

APAG Hobbies Inc.
2470-B North Glassell St.
Orange, CA 92665

Aristo-Polk's International
314 Fifth Ave.
New York, NY 10001

Atlas Tool Co. Inc.
378 Florence Ave.
Hillside, NJ 07205

B.L. Hobby Products
2715 Avalon Dr.
Bettendorf, IA 52722

Camino Scale Models
P.O. Box 10666
Eugene, OR 97401

Custom Brass
(See N.J. International)

**Electronic Specialty
Products (E.S.P.)**
8913 W. Cermak Rd.
North Riverside, IL 60546

GarGraves Trackage Corp.
R.D. #1
North Rose, NY 14516

Hobby Factory Inc.
P.O. Box 67
Abington, PA 19001

Hobby Marketing Inc.
100 Main St.
Reading, MA 01867

Jouef
(See Aristo-Polk's Inter-
national)

Kemtron Corp.
P.O. Box 360
Walnut, CA 91789

LaBelle Industries

P.O. Box 328
Bensenville, IL 60106

Life-Like Products, Inc.
1600 Union Ave.
Baltimore, MD 21211

Merzbach Co. Inc.
200 Fifth Ave.
New York, NY 10010

Minitrix
(See Model Power)

MLR Manufacturing Co.
P.O. Box 1051
Carlsbad, CA 92008

Model Die Casting Inc.
3811 W. Rosecrans Ave.
Hawthorne, CA 90250

Model Power
180 Smith St.
Farmingdale, NY 11735

N.J. International
22 W. Nicholi St.
Hicksville, NJ 11801

"N" Way Products
1650 Mayfield Lane
Madison, WI 53704

Peco
(See Hobby Marketing)

Rail Craft Products
2201 Atwater
St. Louis, MO 63133

Rapido
(See Stevens International)

Roundhouse Products
(See Model Die Casting)

Stevens International
P.O. Box 2908
Cherry Hill, NJ 08034

Tru-Scale Models, Inc.
P.O. Box 8157
Prairie Village, KS 66208

Wabash Valley Lines Inc.
R.R. 2, Sycamore Hollow
Huntington, IN 46750

Wm. K. Walthers Inc.
5601 W. Florist Ave.
Milwaukee, WI 53218

ENVIRONMENTS

A.I.M Products
P.O. Box 5201
Greensboro, NC 27403

Alexander Scale Models
P.O. Box 7121
Grand Rapids, MI 49510

APAG Hobbies, Inc.
2470-B North Glassell St.

Orange, CA 92665

Associated Hobby Manufacturers, Inc.
401 E. Tioga St.
Philadelphia, PA 19134

Athearn, Inc.
1510 W. 135th St.
Gardena, CA 90249

Bachmann Bros. Inc.
1400 Erie Ave.
Philadelphia, PA 19124

Boyd Models
1835 Whittier Ave.
Building B-1
Costa Mesa, CA 92627

Brawa
(See Stevens International)

Campbell Scale Models
P.O. Box 121
Tustin, CA 92680

Classic Miniatures
390 Freeport Blvd., No. 10
Sparks, NV 89431

Color-Rite Scenery Products
2041 Winnetka Ave., North
Minneapolis, MN 55427

Con-Cor
(See JMC International)

Dyna-Model Products Co.
Kemp Road
Sangerville, ME 04479

Fine Scale Miniatures
49 Main St.
Peabody, MA 01960

Hobby Marketing Inc.
Bldg. 4—96-C Commerce Way
Woburn, MA 01801

Holgate & Reynolds
601 Davis St.
Evanston, IL 60201

JMC International
1025 Industrial Drive
Bensenville, IL 60106

John's Lab, Inc.
4915 Dean St.
Woodstock, IL 60098

Jouef
(See Aristo-Polk's International)

K & L House of Wood
P.O. Box 8506
Long Beach, CA 90808

Kadee Quality Products
720 S. Grape St.
Medford, OR 97501

Kibri
(See Hobby Marketing)

Lambert Associates
P.O. Box 4338
San Leandro, CA 94579

Life-Like Products, Inc.
1600 Union Ave.
Baltimore, MD 21211

Lytler & Lytler
Architects in Miniature
2634 Bryant Ave., South
Minneapolis, MN 55408

Magnuson Models
P.O. Box 199
Lake Villa, IL 60046

Malachite Co.
P.O. Box 14223
Fort Worth, TX 76117

Merten
(See Stevens International)

Merzbach Co. Inc.
200 Fifth Ave.
New York, NY 10010

Minitrix
(See Model Power)

MLR Manufacturing Co.
P.O. Box 1051
Carlsbad, CA 92008

Model Die Casting Inc.
3811 W. Rosecrans Ave.
Hawthorne, CA 90250

Model Hobbies
P.O. Box 322
New Cumberland, PA 17070

Model Masterpieces, Ltd.
P.O. Box 1634
Englewood, CO 80110

Model Power
180 Smith St.
Farmingdale, NY 11735

Mountains in Minutes
I.S.L.E. Laboratories
Sylvania, OH 43560

Muir Models, Inc.
2020M S. Susan St.
Santa Ana, CA 92704

Northeastern Scale Models Inc.
P.O. Box 425
Methuen, MA 01844

Period Miniatures
P.O. Box 1332
Hawthorne, CA 90250

Quality Craft Models Inc.
177 Wheatley Ave.
Northumberland, PA 17857

Railhead
P.O. Box 91276
Los Angeles, CA 90009

Revell Inc.
4223 Glencoe Ave.
Venice, CA 90291

Scale Railway Equipment Co.
2010 Elkins Dr.
St. Louis, MO 63136

Scale Structures Ltd.
710 Redwood Place
Reno, NV 89502

Stevens International
P.O. Box 2908
Cherry Hill, NJ 08034

E. Suydam & Co.
P.O. Box 55
Duarte, CA 91010

Tru-Scale Models, Inc.
P.O. Box 8157
Prairie Village, KS 66208

Twinn-K Inc.
P.O. Box 31228
10296 W. Washington St.
Indianapolis, IN 46231

Tyco Industries Inc.
540 Glen Ave.
Moorestown, NJ 08057

Vollmer
(See Boyd Models)

Wabash Valley Lines, Inc.
R.R. 2, Sycamore Hollow
Huntington, IN 46750

Wm. K. Walthers Inc.
5601 W. Florist Ave.
Milwaukee, WI 53218

Weston
(See Campbell Scale)

Woodland Scenics
P.O. Box 266
Shawnee Mission, KS 66201

POWER PACKS AND WIRING

Acme Model Engineering Co.
654 Bergen Blvd.
Ridgefield, NJ 07657

Aristo-Polk's International
314 Fifth Ave.
New York, NY 10001

Atlas Tool Co. Inc.
378 Florence Ave.
Hillside, NJ 07205

Autopulse
(See Troller)

Bachmann Bros. Inc.
1400 Erie Ave.
Philadelphia, PA 19124

BL Hobby Products
2715 Avalon Dr.
Bettendorf, IA 52722

Electronic Specialty Products (E.S.P.)
8913 W. Cermak Rd.
North Riverside, IL 60546

Heathkit
Heath Co.
Benton Harbor, MI 49022

Hobby Factory Inc.
P.O. Box 67
Abington, PA 19001

Hobby Marketing Inc.
Bldg. 4—96-C Commerce Way
Woburn, MA 01801

Kemtron Corp.
P.O. Box 360
Walnut, CA 91789

LaBelle Industries
P.O. Box 328
Bensenville, IL 60106

L.G.B. National Sales Office
P.O. Box 1247
Milwaukee, WI 53201

Life-Like Products, Inc.
1600 Union Ave.
Baltimore, MD 21211

L.M. Industries
772 E. 53rd St.
Brooklyn, NY 11203

Marnold
(See Walthers)

Model Power
180 Smith St.
Farmingdale, NY 11735

Model Rectifier Corp. (MRC)
2500 Woodbridge Ave.
Edison, NJ 08817

Modeltronics
P.O. Box 9763
Arnold, MD 21012

N.J. International
22 W. Nicholi St.
Hicksville, NY 11801

Pacific Fast Mail (PFM)
P.O. Box 57
Edmonds, WA 98020

Peerless Industries, Inc.
561 Hosmer St.
Marlboro, MA 01752

Power Systems, Inc.
56 Bellis Circle
Cambridge, MA 02140

Reeves International
1107 Broadway
New York, NY 10010

Scott Hobby Systems
P.O. Box 90
Monroe, CT 06468

E. Suydam & Co.
P.O. Box 55
Duarte, CA 91010

Troller Corp.
4445 N. Ravenswood
Chicago, IL 60640

Tyco Industries, Inc.
540 Glen Ave.
Moorestown, NJ 08057

Universal Powermaster Corp.
214 Golden Lane
New Oxford, PA 17350

Western Railcraft
13238 N. 28th St.
Phoenix, AZ 85032

SCRATCH-BUILDING MATERIALS

Alexander Scale Models
P.O. Box 7121
Grand Rapids, MI 49510

APAG Hobbies Inc.
2470-B North Glassell St.
Orange, CA 92665

Athearn, Inc.
1510 W. 135th St.
Gardena, CA 90249

Camino Scale Models
P.O. Box 10666
Eugene, OR 97401

Campbell Scale Models
P.O. Box 121
Tustin, CA 92680

Central Valley Model Works
13000 Saticoy St.
North Hollywood, CA 91605

Detail Associates
P.O. Box 3052
Monterey, CA 93940

Details West
P.O. Box 5132
Hacienda Heights, CA 91745

Durango Press
P.O. Box 512
Manhattan Beach, CA 90266

Dyna-Model Products Co.
Kemp Road
Sangerville, ME 04479

Evergreen Scale Models
1717 N.E. 92nd St.
Seattle, WA 98115

Grandt Line Products
2709 Las Armas
Oakland, CA 94611

Hobby Marketing Inc.
Bldg. 4—96-C Commerce Way
Woburn, MA 01801

Holgate & Reynolds
601 Davis St.
Evanston, IL 60201

JMC International
1025 Industrial Drive
Bensenville, IL 60106

Kadee Quality Products
720 S. Grape St.
Medford, OR 97501

Kemtron Corp.
P.O. Box 360
Walnut, CA 91789

Keystone Locomotive Works
159 Wheatley Ave.
Northumberland, PA 17857

K & S Engineering
6917 W. 59th St.
Chicago, IL 60638

LaBelle Industries
P.O. Box 328
Bensenville, IL 60106

Menzies Co.
P.O. Box 153
Silverton, OR 97381

Model Masterpieces Ltd.
P.O. Box 1634
Englewood, CO 80110

Model Traction Supply Co.
P.O. Box 50
Middletown, NY 10940

M.V. Products
P.O. Box 6622
Orange, CA 92667

N.J. International
22 W. Nicholi St.
Hicksville, NY 11801

Northeastern Scale Models
P.O. Box 425
Methuen, MA 01844

Northwest Short Lines
P.O. Box 423
Seattle, WA 98111

Period Miniatures
P.O. Box 1332
Hawthorne, CA 90250

Plastruct, Inc.
1161 Monterey Pass Rd.
Monterey Park, CA 91754

Precision Scale Co.
Rt. 1, Box 1802
Davis, CA 95616

Quality Craft Models Inc.
177 Wheatley Ave.
Northumberland, PA 17857

Rail Line Co.
3600 Pitmann Rd.
Independence, MO 64052

Roller Bearing Models (RBM)
P.O. Box 573
Livingston, NJ 07039

Scale Structures Ltd.
710 Redwood Place
Reno, NV 89502

E. Suydam & Co.
P.O. Box 55
Duarte, CA 91010

Wabash Valley Lines Inc.
R.R. 2, Sycamore Hollow
Huntington, IN 46750

TOOLS AND SUPPLIES

Ambroid Co. Inc.
P.O. Box 1089
Taunton, MA 02780

Badger Air-Brush Co.
9128 W. Belmont Ave.
Franklin Park, IL 60131

Bammco
P.O. Box 1334
Canoga Park, CA 91304

Dixon Co.
750 Washington Ave.
Carlstadt, NJ 07072

Dremel Manufacturing
4915 21st St.
Racine, WI 53406

Duro Art Supply Co.
1832 Juneway Terrace
Chicago, IL 60626

F.A.I. Model Supply
1800 W. Hatcher Rd.
Phoenix, AZ 85021

Floquil
Route 30 North
Amsterdam, NY 12010

Griffin Manufacturing Co.
1656 Ridge Rd.
East Webster, NY 14580

Grumbacher Inc.
460 W. 34th St.
New York, NY 10001

Hobsco Inc.
P.O. Box 18133
Milwaukee, WI 53218

K & S Engineering
6917 W. 59th St.
Chicago, IL 60638

Kemtron Corp.
P.O. Box 360
Walnut, CA 91789

Krasel Industries Inc.
1821 E. Newport Circle
Santa Ana, CA 92705

LaBelle Industries
P.O. Box 328
Bensenville, IL 60106

Loew-Cornell Inc.
131 W. Ruby Ave.
Palisades Park, NJ 07650

Merit Modular Products
P.O. Box 481
Englewood, CO 80151

Microflame Inc.
3724 Oregon Ave., South
Minneapolis, MN 55426

Miller Corp.
2401 Gardner Rd.
Broadview, IL 60153

Model Rectifier Corp. (MRC)
2500 Woodbridge Ave.
Edison, NJ 08817

Moyco
21st & Clearfield Sts.
Philadelphia, PA 19132

Northwest Short Lines
P.O. Box 423
Seattle, WA 98111

Paasche Airbrush Co.
1909 W. Diversey Pkwy.
Chicago, IL 60614

Pactra Industries Inc.
7060 Hollywood Blvd.
Los Angeles, CA 90028

Perma Frost
377 Route 17
Hasbrouck Heights, NJ 07604

Permanent Pigments
1100 Church Lane
Easton, PA 18042

Po Instrument Co.
13 Lehigh Ave.
Paterson, NJ 07503

Precision Manufacturing Co.
4546 Sinclair Rd.
San Antonio, TX 78222

Quality Craft Models Inc.
177 Wheatley Ave.
Northumberland, PA 17857

Scalecoat
(See Quality Craft Models)

Testor Corp.
620 Buckbee St.
Rockford, IL 61101

Twinn-K Inc.
P.O. Box 31228
10296 W. Washington St.
Indianapolis, IN 46231

X-Acto
45-35 Van Dam St.
Long Island City, NY 11101

Advice from the Experts

The more deeply you delve into the hobby of model railroading, the more experts you'll find who are willing to share what they've learned.

By joining a club or by reading some of the publications directed toward model railroaders, you'll be able to pick up tips from these experts on ways to improve a train's operation, methods of decorating cars and surrounding scenery, and advice on every other aspect of the hobby.

During the years that they've been involved with the hobby, advanced hobbyists have invented and perfected techniques that can be of great value to all fans of replica trains. The tips illustrated on the following pages have been accumulated from a variety of sources to give you an idea of the model railroader's ingenuity.

Epoxy and cyanoacrylate (super) glues are excellent substitutes for solder when you need a very strong bond. But be careful, because they can often bond your fingers together instantly. Read the directions carefully.

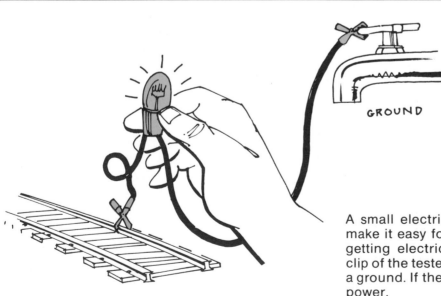

A small electric tester with a 12-volt bulb can make it easy for you to determine if the track is getting electricity. Simply attach one alligator clip of the tester to the track and the other clip to a ground. If the bulb lights, the track is receiving power.

Goldenrod, picked in the autumn, can be used to simulate many different types of trees. If your layout calls for trees in their fall colors, paint the plant with yellow, red and orange tempera paints.

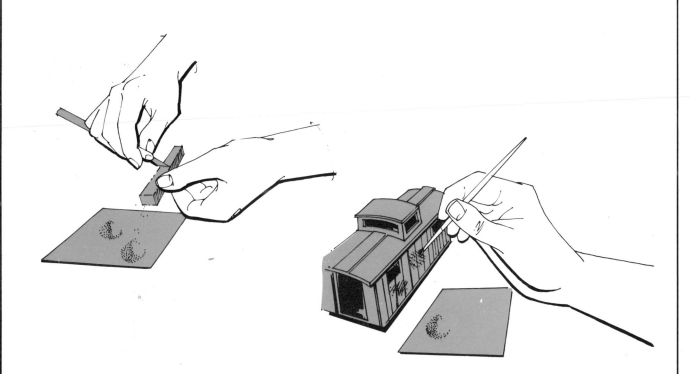

You can use colored chalk to weather your entire model train. Buy a selection of colored pastels in light and dark brown, red, white, dark blue and green. Scrape each piece of chalk with a hobby knife until you have a small pile of each color on a piece of paper. Next, make a "snub brush" by cutting off the front section of bristles of an artist's brush, leaving only stiff, short bristles. Spray the model with dull-coat spray fixative, tap the snub brush into the desired color of chalk dust, and smudge the color onto the model. Then give a final coat of spray fixative.

You can experiment with different types of plants to duplicate particular kinds of trees. When you find one that is suitable, preserve it by dipping the plant in shellac. Then spray with flat green paint.

Good tree frames can be made from hedge clippings. Glue lichen (available in hobby shops) onto the frame to complete the tree.

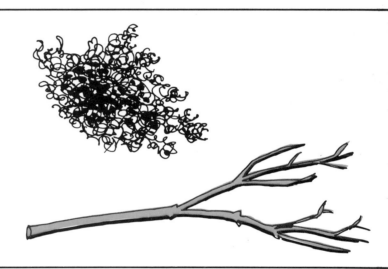

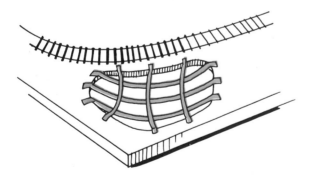
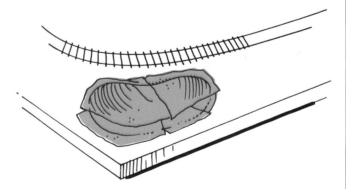
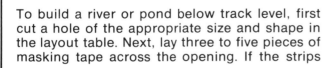

To build a river or pond below track level, first cut a hole of the appropriate size and shape in the layout table. Next, lay three to five pieces of masking tape across the opening. If the strips sag, you're doing it right. Then dip strips of paper towel in plaster, and lay them over the masking tape. When the plaster is dry, you have a foundation for building the body of water.

Heavy train cars stay on the track better. You can add weight to them by pouring melted bismuth alloys—which, because of their low melting point, won't harm plastics—into the cars. Or you can use plaster of paris, plastic wood or wax mixed with lead shot to add the desired weight. Be careful not to add so much weight that the train's performance suffers.

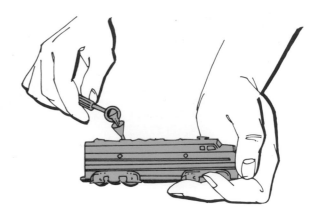

Access hatches are necessary on large layouts that locate parts of the scenery and track out of arm's reach. These are simply sections about 18 inches square that either lift out of the layout or swing down or up out of the way. You can reach derailed trains and perform maintenance tasks by crawling under the table and coming up through the hatch. Don't forget to conceal the juncture of the hatch and the rest of the layout. Concealment can be done with lichen, or by building an obstruction in the line of sight of the viewer.

Working on wiring under the layout table can be a lot easier if you construct a "creeper." It can be made from an old chair seat or a heavy board. Attach either furniture casters or low-profile creeper wheels, available in auto parts stores. A tool tray is a nice finishing touch, since your tools will move with you as you glide from one position to another.

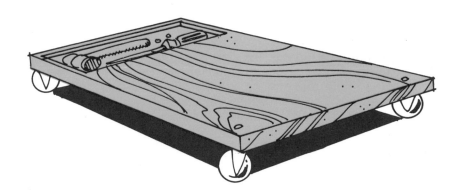

The drying time of plaster of paris or patching plaster can be lengthened by adding a small amount of vinegar to the plaster mixture. A few drops per quart is adequate.

Crepe hair, used for theatrical beards and mustaches, can simulate weeds and brush on a model train layout. It's available from theatrical supply houses and costume stores.

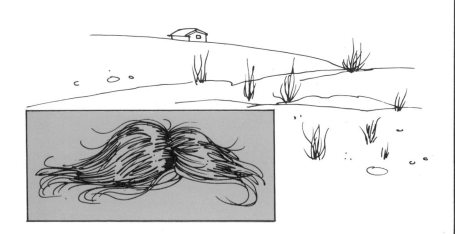

If you notice that your smoke locomotive is not producing adequate smoke, the smoke unit may need cleaning. Dirt and smoke material may be clogging the stack and the smoke generator's tiny air opening. Use a cotton-tipped swab to clean the stack. Then place the locomotive on the track and lift slightly, so that the wheels can spin. Run the locomotive at high speed for a few minutes. This should clean everything out and solve the problem.

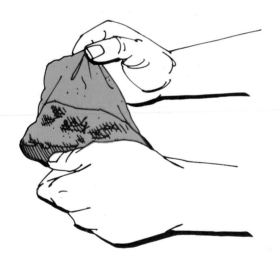

The best way to reproduce rock textures is to make castings of actual rocks. These are made with liquid latex, available in hobby shops. First, find a piece of rock with the desired texture. Then clean the surface with a wire brush. Next, wet the rock well. While the rock is still wet, brush on the liquid latex, making sure it flows into all crevices. Give the rock about eight coatings, letting each coat dry before the next application. When the last coat is dry, peel the mold away. From this mold you can make a plaster casting that can be applied to the scenery when dry, or applied while still wet and held in place while the casting dries.

When assembling model trains, keep a small amount of beeswax handy. If you encounter a tiny screw that's difficult to start by hand, put some wax in the screw slot and insert the screwdriver. The wax will hold the driver head in the slot, enabling you to start the screw easily.

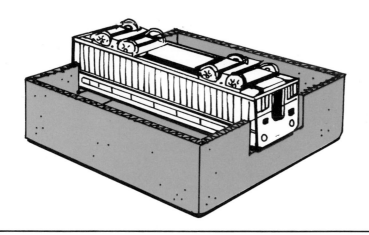

Working on the underside of a model railroad car or locomotive is easier if you have a model holder. Simply cut two slots in a cardboard box, as shown in the illustration.

Real wire looks unrealistic when used for telephone wires, and it is difficult to work with. Use cotton sewing thread instead. It looks good and is easy to position and repair.

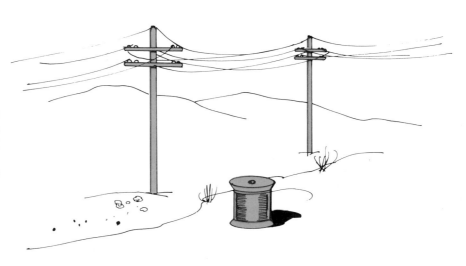

Traction on grades can be increased by rubbing ordinary white chalk on one rail or by scraping emery paper across the track rails.

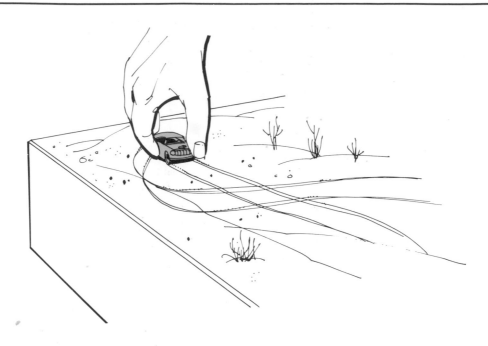

Dirt roads can be made using plaster and bird gravel. First, apply the plaster to the layout where the road is to run. Before the plaster dries, run a model car over the road several times to make wheel ruts like those that appear on real dirt roads. Make sure the model car is the same scale as your train, and crisscross the ruts for a realistic effect. Then apply bird gravel and paint the gravel a color that's close to the adjacent soil on your layout.

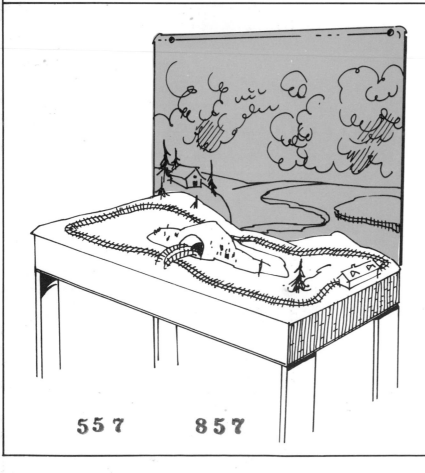

Backdrops add much to the realism of your layout. You can use commercial backdrops or photomurals, or paint your own if you are artistic. In any case, make sure the backdrop matches the scene of your layout closely. Roads that lead from the layout table to a tunnel, road or bridge on the backdrop must blend in well to produce one desirable effect.